COMPULSIONS

COMPULSIONS

How to Stop Doing
What You <u>Don't</u> Want to Do!

by Dr. Joan Lakin
and Caroline Whiting

PRICE STERN SLOAN
Los Angeles

Published by Price Stern Sloan, Inc.
11150 Olympic Boulevard, Suite 650, Los Angeles, California 90064
Printed in U.S.A.
9 8 7 6 5 4 3 2 1

Book produced by
Summerlin Publishing Group
P.O. Box 32012, Tucson, Arizona 85751-2012

Library of Congress Cataloging-in-Publication Data

Lakin, Joan
    Compulsions / by Joan Lakin and Caroline Whiting.
        p. cm.
    Includes index.
    ISBN 0-8431-2917-4
    1. Compulsive behavior. I. Whiting, Caroline M. II. Title.
RC533.L25 1991
616.85'227—dc20   90-21597
                                                                        CIP

Although the names of all the author's clients who are discussed in this book have been changed to protect their identities, as have their descriptions and the identifying characteristics of their stories, the compulsions depicted in this book are recounted from real personal histories. The circumstances surrounding the compulsive behaviors have been adapted to accurately illustrate the nature of compulsions, their debilitating effects and the process that has helped so many to reclaim their lives.

This book has been printed on acid-free paper.

Contents

Foreword

Our world shrinks rapidly as media communication accelerates and information is shared more immediately. Years ago Buckminster Fuller (who coined the word *synergy*) observed me presenting a session of the Rubenfeld Synergy Method, a process I created that allows one to contact, express and work through body tensions and stored emotions by using touch and subtle movements. Smiling, he said, "Ilana, you have demonstrated that your work truly treats a person as a 'whole' because your method has elegantly integrated the body, mind, emotions and spirit in a synergistic way." (*Synergism* is defined in the *American Heritage Dictionary of the English Language* as "the action of two or more substances, organs or organisms to achieve an effect of which each is individually incapable." My method involves the synergism of the mind and body.) Now Joan Lakin has taken the theories and practices of the Rubenfeld Synergy Method and woven them into the fabric of her work with people who find themselves shackled by the bonds of compulsive behavior patterns.

The immediacy and authenticity that characterize the work of Joan Lakin are not accidental. For Joan herself has travelled the pathway on which she has been a guide for so many of her clients. I have known Dr. Lakin for fifteen years, initially as a member of my first Rubenfeld Synergy Training program, then as senior faculty member on my training staff and finally as a respected and trusted colleague. Joan was loved by the trainees because she approached each one with compassion, patience, skill and clarity. Yet she was always herself, sharing some of her own process and life experiences when appropriate.

In one of my earliest memories of Joan, I recall her staring with longing at a luscious chocolate cake that was being passed around among the staff members. Although Joan's body language revealed her craving for chocolate, she stalwartly refused a piece. Later Joan told the group that she was afflicted with a powerful longing for chocolate, a longing so pervasive that she would literally eat huge portions of chocolate until her mind couldn't think clearly. Having already embarked on her own recovery process, she asked our staff to support her by developing an approach in which we were to intervene with questions and actions so that she could stop and listen to her body and her feelings. Joan's habitual consumption of chocolate was like *all* habitual behavior in that we have *no* choice over it. Watching Joan move from compulsive eating habits to a stance of choice about her treatment of her body was a great joy for me.

One of the significant contributions that the Rubenfeld Synergy Method has made to Joan's personal and professional life is its contention that the body mirrors our internal states; it portrays the feelings, beliefs and attitudes we hold. The body does not lie; it presents a strikingly honest picture of whatever is out of harmony in our system if we are willing to listen to its wisdom.

As I read the personal recovery stories in this book, I noted how skillfully Joan incorporated the principles of the Rubenfeld Synergy Method into her practice. First, the person is treated as a whole being—mind, body and emotions. Second, the body is viewed as a metaphor that reveals as much as words. Third, the spirit of nonviolence, gentleness and empathy (never forcing individuals to reveal themselves before they are ready) is essential. Fourth, self-care is an essential component of recovery. Joan models physical and emotional health for clients who are often out of touch with their own self-care. Fifth, attention to the adult and the inner child is extremely important because it is often the damaged and deprived child within who desperately needs physical and emotional feeding. Joan skillfully addresses both the adult and the child, creating a safe environment in which her clients can explore the roots of their compulsive behavior patterns.

"Why do I do it? Why can't I stop it?" These are agonizing questions asked by thousands of people who find themselves imprisoned by compulsive behavior patterns. This book addresses these painful and urgent questions in a clear, warm and methodical way. The straightforward, conversational tone used by the authors invites us to witness the unfolding therapeutic process as we read the poignant case histories of Dr. Lakin's clients. Here is a book full of help for those who wish to use their compulsive behavior as a starting position on a journey toward health, integration and creative choice.

Ilana Rubenfeld, M.A.
President and Executive Director
The Rubenfeld Center, Inc.

Acknowledgments

First of all, I would like to acknowledge my coauthor, Caroline Whiting, whose talent and commitment gave voice to my material. I couldn't have imagined a more creative partnership.

I would also like to acknowledge my two children, Lisa and Garret, whose supportive enthusiasm helped me to have more fun; Dagmar O'Connor, for her generosity and guiding hand; and my teacher and mentor, Ilana Rubenfeld.

Thanks also to Nancy Torek, whose perfect WordPerfect® skills and impeccable typing enabled us to meet our deadline.

Joan Lakin

Introduction

One night as I turned on the news, I was startled to hear that a leading American educator had been charged with making anonymous obscene phone calls to a young woman who lived in the area. Further investigation revealed that for some years he had been the victim of a secret, agonizing compulsion over which he had had no control. The irresistible impulse to pick up the phone and utter obscenities into the ear of a young female was stronger than his willpower, stronger than the possibility of losing his reputation or destroying his family.

This educator, who proved to be a courageous, empathetic person, eventually shared his story with the public in the hope that he could help others who suffered from similar afflictions. He revealed that he had been sexually abused as a child, that he had recently received treatment for his problem, that he deeply regretted hurting anyone and that he was moving ahead with his life.

Not all of us have such agonizing and overt afflictions. Some of us cannot sleep if the dishes are still in the sink, some of us should not be let loose in the mall with charge cards and some of us think the company will fold if we don't put in thirteen hours a day at work.

If you find yourself unable to resist occasional—or frequent—overwhelming impulses, if you wonder where your unpredictable, irrational acts suddenly come from, this book is for you. You are not alone; thousands of men and women struggle with uncontrollable behaviors that cost them time, money, energy, resources and their emotional and/or physical well-being.

But there is help. Scores of my clients have turned their lives around as a result of the process outlined in this book. This book is about the struggles of people, all clients or former clients of mine, whose lives were driven by compulsive behaviors—and how they got better. One couldn't pass a movie theater without going in, another spent thousands of dollars she didn't have at the casinos in Atlantic City, a third lived the pampered life of a dazzling seductress, for which she forfeited true intimacy and affection.

As the stories of these clients—and those of numerous other clients with a whole range of compulsive behaviors—unfold before you in these pages, you will see how the debilitating effects of their compulsions devastated their personal and professional lives—until they got help. When they discovered that their compulsive behaviors were clues to past traumas that still ran their lives, when they uncovered the tempestuous, painful feelings that lay buried beneath their carefully constructed facades, when they became aware of the family trance that had unwitting held each of them under its spell, they started to get better. They saw that their compulsive behavior came from an identifiable source, operated in a predictable pattern, and could be alleviated with a steadfast commitment to the step-by-step process of awareness, clarification, and recovery presented in the chapters that follow.

These clients got better, and you can, too. But nothing worth having comes without hard work. As Pulitzer Prize-winning author Annie Dillard has written in her book *The Writing Life,* "It is handed to you, but only if you look for it." She was talking about the gift of writing. But the same thing is true of any creative process, including the crafting of our lives. Finally, any insight that strikes us, any change that happens to us, comes gratuitously. But we have to struggle for it first.

There are several ways you can read this book. One is to get information about an interesting topic. A second is to see if you find yourself mirrored in the lives of the people whose stories I tell. A third is to use it as a program that will enable you to move toward greater awareness, choice and creativity in your own life. Yet a fourth is to use it in all three ways.

For whatever reason you read this book, I welcome you to join me on an adventure that's well worth the potential risk.

PART ONE

Irresistible Impulses, Irrational Acts

CHAPTER ONE

Compulsions: Mood-Altering Behaviors That Control Your Life

Harry quickened his pace as he approached the busy intersection. He wanted to get across before the light changed, leaving him stuck on the corner. If he didn't cross the wide, congested street immediately, he might not cross at all. Harry was acutely aware that just down the block from where he was standing there was a cinema that was featuring a new release.

Just like an alcoholic who knows the location of every bar in town, Harry knew where all the movie theaters were. He also knew that if he made a mistake and turned down the wrong street, he would be irretrievably enticed into the cool, dark interior of an inviting theater. Like a giant magnet, the cinema would draw him right in, holding him inside its powerful force field for hours as he passively sat, mesmerized by sound and image.

Harry was a movie binger. Sometimes, calling in sick with yet another made-up illness, he would start in the morning, as soon as the theaters opened. Sometimes—if he could get away with it—he would stay in one cinema all day, viewing the same show three or four times, until he knew entire portions of dialogue by heart. Occasionally he would hide from the ushers, waiting for the cover of darkness to blanket him with anonymity once again. Or he might migrate from theater to theater, seeing a comedy, then a thriller and finally a love story.

After he emerged from the temporary oblivion he fell into during his binge, Harry would feel an acute sense of loss at the hours that had slipped by without his noticing, days that had vanished as he sat staring at the screen, watching others live their lives while his remained unlived. But he felt powerless over his compulsion.

◊◊◊

Tears welled up in Monica's wide brown eyes and trickled down her cheeks, leaving little white trails through her raspberry-colored blush. Nervously she twisted a single strand of chestnut hair round and round her forefinger. "This time," she began, "it happened after I saw my sister's scissors lying next to the sewing machine. I just thought I'd snip off this one uneven piece here." She pointed to a sawed-off lock near her right temple. "By then it was too late," she continued. "I kept thinking one more cut would even it all out—and now look!"

This wasn't the first time Monica had shown up for an appointment designer-attired and impeccably groomed—except for a ragged, gaminlike hairstyle. The crowning glory that so many women cleverly turn to their own cosmetic advantage was a source of despair to Monica. She would see her shadow on the wall. One little hair would be out of place, so she'd cut it off. Other strands would look uneven, and she'd trim them. She'd force herself to stay in her office instead of bolting for home—to the large bathroom mirror and the ample light—in pursuit of that elusive perfect coiffure.

During weekend shopping expeditions Monica began to avoid fabric shops, hardware stores and any other place where rows of gleaming stainless scissors beckoned her to pick them up and start shearing. Occasionally she even locked up her office scissors in the top right-hand desk drawer and put the key in the saucer under the potted plant down the hall.

Like so many of my other clients, Harry and Monica suffered from compulsive behaviors that made their daily lives painful and chaotic. But there is a rhyme and reason to compulsions—even though we may not know what it is at first. Compulsions serve as clues to the deeper stories of our lives, and if, like good sleuths, we are tenacious and work hard, we can unravel the mysteries to which compulsions are the clues, as Harry and Monica did.

Compulsions as Clues in Our Personal Mystery Stories

When my children were of elementary-school age, we used to play Clue, a Parker Brothers game that brought hours of amusement to the whole family. The point of Clue was to track down, from among a number of possibilities, the particulars of a murder. Who did it? What was the murder weapon? Where was the crime committed? Did Professor Plum do it in the kitchen with a knife? Or did Mrs. White do it in the library with a wrench? After gathering enough clues on the murder mystery trail to hazard a keenly calculated guess, someone would shout excitedly, "I got it! Miss Scarlet did it in the living room with an ax!" We would check the secret cards, which had been selected randomly and hidden in an envelope at the beginning of the game. If, indeed, Miss Scarlet had done it in the living room with an ax, then the game would be over and justice would have been served.

Each of our lives is a great human mystery story—although fortunately, for most of us, the tale does not culminate in murder. As a therapist, I have the priceless opportunity to participate in many living mystery stories, stories of tragedy, pathos, wonder, joy and endurance—but most of all, of the infinite possibility and unpredictability of human life. By being invited into the stories of my clients, I have embarked upon a particular kind of mystery trail in my professional capacity as a therapist.

In my practice I began to notice that compulsive behaviors were afflicting a large number of the men and women I worked with. These behaviors were self-defeating, debilitating and sometimes even disabling. What I have discovered is that a compulsion is a clue to an individual's history of emotional woundedness. By working with it, observing it, analyzing it and taking it seriously, one can uncover and virtually reexperience the scarred emotional history that is compressed into a routinized behavior pattern. The compulsion serves as the first clue on a mystery trail that leads to the root of a person's psychic distress.

The process of clue gathering usually has two levels. First, in many cases involving common, fairly ordinary compulsive behaviors, the people who engage in these behaviors have no idea that they are behaving compulsively. Their compulsions are so intertwined with their everyday behavior that they have no perspective or distance from which to see them, no consciousness of them. In these cases, the first part of the clue-gathering process is becoming aware that a compulsive behavior exists. In the case of more extreme, obvious compulsions such as shoplifting or gambling, the compulsive behavior may be hard to conceal from oneself or others.

As soon as we are aware that a compulsive behavior exists, the second level of clue gathering begins. The compulsion itself is a clue to the existence of a core belief system that we unconsciously live by. Just as the tip indicates the presence of an iceberg, so the compulsive behavior reveals the model of reality that governs our lives. By unraveling the story line the compulsion points to, we can eventually name and confront the source of psychic distress. The journey we take toward this destination is full of surprises, detours and difficult terrain. Sometimes the trail seems to disappear altogether. But if we persist, we will always arrive at our destination. If we stay with the process of unraveling the story, we will come face to face with that which our compulsion masked—the wound we wanted to avoid. It is only by confronting, naming and knowing this wound that we can move toward recovery.

What Is a Compulsion?

A *compulsion* is a behavior that is habitually reenacted in order to alter a mood, to transform a bad feeling into a good feeling. Virtually anything can become a compulsion—exercising, spending, flirting, going to movies, eating chocolates or speeding on freeways. A compulsion covers up an interior emptiness. It indicates the presence of a control mechanism—a way of escaping something that is ultimately inescapable and unavoidable.

The behaviors seen in common compulsions are not usually in themselves inappropriate. Rather, it is the way they are used and what they are used for that creates a problem. A normal, natural behavior such as eating or shopping becomes compulsive when it is misordered, unprioritized or inappropriate to the circumstances. The grasping, driven, insistent quality that is the earmark of a compulsion is easily detected in the compulsive winner engaging in a heated argument or in the shopper charging purchases that she can never pay for.

As mood alterers, compulsions represent attempts to compensate for the feelings of low self-esteem and powerlessness that beset people in deep emotional pain. The immediate agenda of a compulsion is to maintain a sense of basic survival in the face of what feels like certain annihilation. The usual priorities of normal life become irrelevant in the presence of the overwhelming fear, guilt and shame that threaten the core of one's being. Seen as a survival mechanism, a compulsive spending spree in the wake of a severed relationship makes perfect sense. The fundamental, unconscious belief system of the compulsive shopper is that buying will restore shattered self-esteem, autonomy, power and control. Such an unrealistic belief signals the presence of a fantasy that the compulsive person carefully, but unconsciously, constructs as a bulwark in the presence of an untrustworthy reality. This fantasy becomes a beloved companion, a constant presence. Within the gauzelike wrap the fantasy provides, one feels safe, esteemed, secure. The fantasy may be the only security one experiences, and one is loath to give it up.

Characteristics of People with Compulsions

Because of their intense feelings of precariousness in the world, people with compulsions have a strong need for reinforcement. Since engaging in a compulsive behavior seems to offer relief from this tenuousness, the behavior may be repeated again and again—or it may be needed only occasionally. The frequency of repetition depends on the depth of one's pain and/or one's current difficulties in life.

Perhaps the most pervasive characteristic of all of us who have compulsions is that we are out of touch with our real feelings, the feelings that are driving our self-defeating behaviors. Because these hidden feelings are so painful that they cannot be admitted to consciousness, we learn to focus on an external mechanism, such as excessive telephoning, shopping or gambling, which keeps us increasingly out of touch emotionally. To reinforce the stance we've taken—that is, hiding out from our real feelings—we employ all kinds of defenses, particularly denial, rationalization and control. Since acknowledging our real feelings would blow our cover and admit into awareness the inadmissible, we learn to control our feelings through our compulsive behaviors.

Engaging in a compulsive activity creates the feeling of momentary control, with the illusion of eternal control. In the compulsive act, the sensation of power and excitement functions as a switch to turn on the unconscious fantasy of being all-powerful and totally safe. But the reality is that a compelled person is driven and out of control. The paradox is that, even as we telephone or gamble or shop, thus feeling in control, we are absolutely out of control. The desperate need to control the uncontrollable feelings creates the compulsion, which creates the illusion of control, which keeps us stuck, without authentic control. Thus those of us with compulsions become trapped inside a vicious circle of our own creation. The illusions we create to save ourselves become the proverbial wolves in sheeps' clothing. In pursuing our illusions, we create our own betrayal.

Compulsions and Addictions: Similarities and Differences

Compulsions and addictions are both concerned with mood alteration. They are attempts to generate a sense of well-being from an external source rather than from within. Although compulsions and addictions can have similar effects on human lives, they differ greatly from each other. The term *compulsion*, as I shall use it throughout this book, refers to a specific, reactive behavior that temporarily brings about a sense of power, control, self-esteem and security. (See the earlier definition on page 5.) An *addiction*, on the other hand, alters a mood as a result of one's ingesting a substance that is immediately toxic to the body. Heroin, cocaine, crack and the many other harmful substances commonly used in our society have immediately toxic effects on our systems and are life-threatening—sooner or later.

PHYSIOLOGICAL EFFECTS

Even the milder addictive substances our culture relies on for stimulation and relaxation have toxic effects on our bodies. Medical authorities point out that smoking cigarettes destroys platelets, constricts blood vessels and is associated with cancer of the lungs and other organs. It is well known that alcohol consumption kills brain cells. And Sadja Greenwood, assistant clinical professor at the University of California Medical Center, warns in her book *Menopause Naturally* that heavy caffeine use increases blood pressure and has been connected with heart disease and elevated levels of serum cholesterol. These substances are inherently dangerous to our health and well-being. In varying degrees, all of them threaten our health and well-being. Their use involves a physiological component—that is, ingestion of a toxic substance—that does not characterize compulsive behaviors.

It is true that compulsive behaviors involve physiological changes; they would not be able to alter moods if they did not produce chemical changes in the body. These physiological changes are often perceived as a "rush," such as that produced by the increased heart rate of a speeder doing ninety miles an hour. A number of compulsive behaviors may even constitute life-threatening patterns. For example, cruising freeways at high speeds can kill or maim, and compulsive eating may contribute to heart disease or cancer of the colon. However, the behavior itself (that is, speeding or eating) is not inherently negative or life-threatening. Using a charge card to make a purchase or flirting with office co-workers isn't intrinsically debilitating. It's the misordered, driven aspect of the behavior in one's personality structure—and the resulting chemical changes inside the body—that cause a problem.

Our everyday language reflects the distinction between compulsions and addictions. We hear people refer to "compulsive shoppers" or "compulsive eaters" and to "cocaine addicts." Shopping and eating are normal, necessary human behaviors, whereas using cocaine is not. Ingesting, shooting up or snorting drugs are not, by any normal standards, inherently natural behaviors.

Although eating destructively is a compulsive behavior, I will not deal with compulsive food consumption at length in this book; there are already a number of helpful books available on eating disorders. The terms "sex addiction" and "relationship addiction" are prevalent today, but neither unhealthy relationships nor unhealthy sexual activities involve the ingestion of toxic substances. Though both may be classified as compulsions, I have not concentrated on relationship "addiction" (often known as *codependency*) in this book because there are already many books on the market in that area. My focus in this book remains exclusively on other behaviors that are used as mood-altering devices.

A COMMON CAUSE

Despite their differences, compulsions and addictions share a common cause: the need to escape from intense psychic pain. However, unlike compulsions, addictions often involve biological predispositions to drugs and alcohol. When people with such predispositions use drugs as medications to dull their pain, their need for emotional anesthetization couples with their genetic predisposition to drugs, causing them to become addicted.

Surprisingly, in certain ways compulsive behaviors are much more insidious than addictions. First of all, many people are oblivious to the fact that debilitating compulsions are dominating their behavior. Their unawareness keeps them enchained. Secondly, the compulsion is usually so intertwined with and inseparable from the personality that it is difficult to discover and slippery to work with.

By contrast, addictions are more obvious because they involve substances that are tangible and visible—to the addict and everyone else. Although abusers are aware that they are ingesting toxic substances, until they break through their denial they are unaware that they are addicts. Denial is essential to addiction; unconsciousness is part of the disease.

PREDICTABLE CYCLES

Finally, both compulsions and addictions follow predictable cycles. Since both patterns have to do with controlling feelings via mood alteration, they aim to create a falsely based sense of power, safety, self-esteem, euphoria. Seduction may bring about a sense of power, alcohol may temporarily appear to eradicate barriers to intimacy and cocaine may create the illusion of euphoria. Whether the mood has been altered by taking a specific action or by ingesting a particular substance, the course the alteration takes is similar. The initial chemical changes in the body escalate and intensify the feelings of well-being and security until they reach a peak, whereupon the tapering off begins, bringing a downswing accompanied by a variety of emotions. The letdown may involve guilt, fear, shame and self-recrimination. The only way out of the letdown is to repeat the pattern via the compulsion or the addiction. The patterns of the cycles vary according to the behavior, the addiction or compulsion and the person.

Let's say that a perky secretary working in the accounting department of a large firm has her eye on an attractive young financial officer. Perhaps she times her arrival at the water cooler on her afternoon break to coincide with his. A charged little interchange ensues, leaving the secretary with a flush of excitement. Her energy level has suddenly escalated, and she feels flushed with excitement. She has momentarily been rescued from the monotony of typing a long statistical report, and she feels validated as a sexually attractive woman. Her flush may last half an hour—maybe more, maybe less. If she wants to re-create the sense of excitement, she will have to engage in the same behavior—sooner or later. If the secretary is compulsive, she will be driven to re-create this experience in inappropriate ways again and again and again. If she is not compulsive, the incident will slide into its appropriate place in her life, functioning as a simple recognition of her innate attractiveness.

As we have noted, the goal of both compulsions and addictions is to climb out of emotional pain by creating illusion-based, temporary mood alterations. In people with addictions, however, after the initial rush feelings tend to be numbed as a result of ingesting the substance. Conversely, in people with compulsions a particular feeling is taken on an escapade and exercised to its limit, again as a way of stuffing unwanted, dangerous feelings below the surface. Thus the flush of sexual excitement the secretary felt may provide the cover-up she needs to avoid awareness of a painful lack of intimacy at home. The intensity of sensation, rather than the anesthetic effects of alcohol, may shield her from unwanted awareness. Although the goal may be similar in compulsions and addictions, the route is somewhat different.

Just as I have distinguished between compulsions and addictions, I want to clarify the difference between the mood-altering compulsions that are the subject of this book and other forms of compulsivity. First, I am not dealing here with the personality type labeled *compulsive* by psychotherapists. This book is not about what is called the *anal-retentive personality,* which is characterized by constant, excessive orderliness, cleanliness and rigidity. It is about normal people who have acquired a repertoire of behaviors that are used frequently, to varying degrees, to alter moods. Nor is this book about the psychopathological, Lady Macbeth-style behaviors termed *obsessive-compulsive* by clinicians. Such behaviors involve hours of repetitive, often physically tortuous rituals such as handwashing, perhaps the most well-known obsessive-compulsive example.

The Cycles of a Compulsion

The goal of a compulsion is establishing a feeling of safety, security and imperviousness to both the real and supposed brutalities of the world. Since each person's need for safety and security is a bit different, each compulsion has its own cyclical variations, depending upon one's personal history and the nature of the compulsion itself. Some people will not engage in their compulsions for weeks or months at a time. The level of their insecurity and fear may not have risen to the danger zone, so they may not feel driven or desperate. Or they may be "white knuckling" it—avoiding compulsive behaviors through sheer force of will, refusing to gamble or shoplift or whatever—until the veneer of their willpower is worn thin and they can control the compulsion no longer.

A particular compulsive pattern may reflect a long period of building up internal pressure before the compulsive behavior is manifested. So patterns may vary—from a steady exercise of compulsive activity to intense cycles that reflect withdrawal from life, a buildup of pressure and acting on the compulsion.

Just as general overall patterns in compulsive activity can be identified, so each compulsive behavior has an identifiable cycle. Simply stated, the cycle consists of the trigger to action, the buildup phase, the peak, the subsequent sense of well-being and the downswing.

AN ILLUSTRATION: VANESSA'S STORY

Vanessa was feeling somewhat despondent. She didn't get the career promotion she interviewed for, she had gained ten pounds from eating at the new pasta place around the corner and life was feeling generally drab. On her way home from work, Vanessa passed by one of the better department stores in town, where the freshly dressed windows revealed some fabulous new spring creations. On an impulse, Vanessa found herself inside, inspecting the costly designer coordinates. Scooping up a few outfits, she spent the next half-hour in the dressing room.

Although she knew perfectly well that she was barely able to meet her monthly charge-card payments, armed with her card for this store, Vanessa purchased a lovely three-piece linen outfit for $600. As she approached the saleswoman at the counter, her sense of exhilaration escalated. Watching as her purchase was rung up on the register, Vanessa anticipated the comments and compliments she'd command with her new outfit. She felt powerful and autonomous as she signed her name on the bottom line of the charge slip.

Heading for the escalator, Vanessa basked in her feelings of decisiveness and control. As she grabbed a cab home, she could hardly wait to model her new outfit for her roommate. The next day at work Vanessa's self-esteem and sense of well-being were fed by compliments from co-workers and even the department chairman.

It wasn't until the next week, when Vanessa sat down with her monthly bills and her bank statement, that the ugly down phase of her shopping expedition began. Filled with panic at the financial picture she saw among the documents on her desk, Vanessa began sliding into guilt, fear and self-recrimination. It was too late to return the merchandise, but how could she ever pay for it?

If this incident had been isolated, it wouldn't have been so traumatic. But Vanessa's department store statements were full of purchases bought on impulse to salve a wounded sense of self-esteem. Her financial picture was a direct reflection of the compulsive cycle that dominated her life. Her irrational, unplanned department store purchases were always attempts to control her feelings, a way of hoisting herself up from an emotional black pit. In her moments of giddy, exhilarated buying, she would forget the feelings of self-loathing that inevitably followed.

THE PHASES OF VANESSA'S COMPULSIVE CYCLE

Vanessa's compulsion reflects the cycle that virtually all compulsions take. First is the trigger to action. A compulsive action can be triggered either externally or internally. A simple stimulus in the environment can prompt a particular compulsive behavior, as it did in Vanessa's case. She simply walked by a department store window and the vision of a beautiful suit triggered her compulsion to buy.

The action may also be caused by a buildup of pressure internally. In this case a compulsive shopper would set out on a shopping spree without being motivated by a particular external display of merchandise. Although the externally prompted buying binge may epitomize the knee-jerk reflex that often characterizes compulsive behavior patterns, both motivations function fairly autonomously. Providing a feeling of power and control, they ride roughshod over the good intentions and willpower of the compelled.

Second, the buildup phase builds on the trigger to action. There is an increase in internal excitement, a sort of sweeping upsurge that seems to gather momentum independent of the person it moves along in its wake. In the case of Vanessa's shopping expedition, the buildup phase was represented by her movement from the store window to the dressing room, where she tried on a number of outfits.

Third, the peak is the phase when the internal movement or buildup culminates in taking action. In the example of Vanessa, it was the actual purchase of her outfit—that is, walking to the cash register and charging the suit with her credit card. The execution of the compulsion, in this case the purchasing, elicits unrealistic feelings of power, control and autonomy. One may feel "on top of the world" as the rush surges into high gear. Because the peak is locatable inside a particular action that usually has a somewhat prescribed time period, it may last only a few seconds or a number of minutes, but not usually longer—unless the cycle is continuously repeated, giving the appearance of one long apex.

The feelings of well-being may extend over a relatively lengthy period. A variety of different illusion-based feelings may be experienced, according to the situation. However, this phase is usually characterized by a sense of total safety, self-esteem, imperviousness to and insulation from the regular vicissitudes of everyday life, security and unaccustomed calmness. This phase may last anywhere from a few minutes to a number of days.

Finally, the downswing of the cycle is an inevitable, although sometimes delayed, part of the compulsive pattern. Often accompanied by feelings of self-loathing, guilt, fear or shame, it is like a horrible personal Judgment Day. The results of our compulsivity come full circle. All the crescendos and euphoric transports are banished by the self-doubt and recrimination we now feel. Vanessa was plummeted into fear, guilt and shame by the state of her finances—feelings she had tried to escape from, ironically, by purchasing the designer suit.

ESCALATION OF THE CYCLE

It is during the down phase that reality starts dangerously intruding into our compulsive life model. In the face of this intrusion, a person in the grip of a compulsion spirals ever more deeply into the bottomless black pit of feelings of worthlessness. It is at this time that we say to ourselves, "How many times do I have to do this? What kind of person am I? See—I thought I was a bad person; now I know it. This proves it. I knew I shouldn't do this, but I did it again anyway. What hope is there for a worthless person like me?"

Paradoxically, in this phase many compulsive people once again exercise their self-defeating behavior patterns, trying to escape the down side of the cycle. Ultimately, of course, this repetition escalates the compulsive pattern to such inflated proportions that we end up courting—and marrying—disaster. For many people, hitting bottom is the only way back up.

Often we have to reach the end of our emotional, financial, relational or spiritual rope before we recognize the cycle and deal with it. But to deal with a compulsion requires that we stop and confront what's driving us. As long as an external behavior mechanism serves as the focus for displaced, hidden feelings, we don't have to look within. The buying, the gambling, the eating, the speeding—all serve as convenient foils that allow us to avoid the real issues.

Confronting the compulsion requires that those of us who are compelled come back to ourselves. But that's what's so difficult—coming back—because what's going on inside hurts so much. So we keep the focus out there, rather than coming back inside and saying, "Wait a moment. How am I really feeling?" To ask that question—let alone to answer it—is like going back to the rubble of a war-torn city. And who wants to go back there?

Facing the Feelings

People in the process of giving up their compulsions almost always find that their lives seem to get worse before they get better. And why not? The compulsion plays a powerful, much-needed role, and it cannot be discarded without what feels like an emotional free-for-all. As one gives up a seduction ritual or a rescuing behavior or a shopping compulsion, all the hidden feelings start to emerge.

Inevitably a client will say to me, "I haven't given way to my compulsion for three weeks—and I feel worse." Of course. The feelings are surfacing, and the process of learning to feel what has been dormant for so long is a painful one, even though the rewards are bountiful. The temptation as the feelings emerge is to be ruled by them, just as a parent caught off guard may give in to the temper tantrums of a volatile two-year-old. But neither controlling the feelings (as we unconsciously attempt to do through the compulsion) nor capitulating to them is beneficial in the long term. Recognizing the feelings, feeling them and externalizing them is an important step along the pathway to recovery.

The ultimate aim is to be able to transfer responsibility for the appropriate expression of feelings to the benevolent, parental part of ourselves, that strong, steady grownup inside of us that is usually developed by having a mature parental model during our childhood years. (If we have no such model in childhood, we have to develop an "inner adult" later in life, which is a hard job indeed.) When we feel driven by the old compulsion, this benevolent parent is able to say, "Oh, I'm feeling that old, empty feeling again. But I can sit with it; I can breathe with it. It's not the end of the world." We can know that, as painful as it may be, it's just a feeling. It may make us uncomfortable or anxious, but it brings a measure of serenity to know that we don't have to be ruled by our momentary feelings of discomfort or even panic. Although I may feel as if I'm going to be annihilated, I know I will not be. When I feel my feeling instead of reacting to it, controlling it or giving in to it, I discover I will survive—without my compulsion.

Fantasy and the Family Trance

As we shall see in Part Three of this book, *Clarification,* compulsions originate in the unconscious construction of a fantasy we create to escape from feelings of powerlessness and pain. Usually the source of these feelings is childhood deprivation of one sort or another. The fantasy, which is complex, intricate and all-encompassing, is often the only solace available in a family situation that is nonsupportive or downright abusive, either emotionally or physically. It becomes the savior, the only consistent, reliable, on-call means a child has to endure his or her individual, silent trauma. And the fantasy is pliable, seemingly responsive to the child's every need, for he creates it as he goes along. Eventually the child responds to his total environment on the basis of this fantasy. Relationships, work situations and ordinary social interactions become the reflections of this illusionary inner world that is based on deprivation and need.

The nature and intensity of one's fantasy is directly related to the dysfunction mirrored in "the family trance"—that is, the model of reality a family lives by. Somewhere along the hard road to recovery from the compulsions that dysfunction breeds, we painfully discover the existence of both the family trance and the fantasy we created in response to it. But in the conscious light of day, what was appropriate to the child is not appropriate to the adult. The fantasy that served the child so well must die, for without its death the adult will forever rely on that fantasy with its illusion of power.

One's lifelong companion cannot die an easy death. One must grieve the loss of the fantasy as if it were a flesh-and-blood friend. Only a conscious mourning process can move one from a childish, stuck orientation to a mature, emotionally sturdy, responsible standpoint.

In the following chapters we shall go through a three-part therapeutic process that will give us the tools to overcome the irresistible impulses and irrational acts that have been undermining, perhaps even destroying, our lives.

PART TWO

Awareness

CHAPTER TWO

Is a Compulsion
Running Your Life?

Once upon a time there was a man who walked to work every day. He would don his suit and tie, down his bowl of bran flakes and cup of black coffee and set out on the mile-long rustic route to his office in the village. Now the roads in this rural community were in disrepair, and there happened to be a giant pothole on the man's route. Every morning as he strode along, deeply absorbed in thought, the man would fall into the pothole—as he had done daily for the last ten years. Upon finding himself underground, he would climb out of the pothole, pick himself up, dust himself off and be on his way.

One day as the man was walking along, enjoying the fine spring weather, he remarked to himself that there was a very large pothole right in his path. Although he actually noticed the size and location of the hole, he nevertheless fell in, according to his habit, whereupon he once again picked himself up and went on his way.

A few days later, as the man again approached the pothole, it suddenly occurred to him that he could, in fact, go around the pothole, saving himself both time and trouble—to say nothing of the money spent at the cleaner's. So the man decided quite deliberately to walk around the pothole, circumventing that portion of his morning ritual. It felt good, not falling in the pothole, and the man thought that the next day he would try walking around it once again.

The following morning, however, the man was pondering the remarks he was going to make at his morning staff meeting, and, totally oblivious to the pothole, he once again fell in. Feeling slightly annoyed with himself, he vowed to watch the road more carefully. Sure enough, the following day, motivated by his desire to stay above ground, the man paid attention and managed to avoid the pothole. As the days and weeks went by, the man gradually increased his attentiveness to the road, managing to stay out of the pothole most mornings. Occasionally, however, lost in his own world, he would slip back into his old habit and find himself suddenly plunged below ground.

Eventually the man found that steering clear of the pothole made his life move so much more smoothly that he wondered how he had ever been so blind as to spend ten years in his old ritual. Although he occasionally had a relapse, finding himself suddenly below ground, he was now able to lead a rewarding, pothole-free life.

◊◊◊

Just as the man in this story was oblivious to his self-defeating routine behavior, so those of us whose lives are governed by compulsive behaviors are unconscious of the control that knee-jerk spending, exercising, seduction, speeding, eating and so on have over us. We are so accustomed to falling into our behavioral potholes that we do not see what we are doing, and it certainly does not occur to us that life can be lived any other way. No change in our behavior can occur until we become aware of that behavior—and of the fact that there are other healthier, saner ways of behaving.

The path to recovery from compulsive behavior is a three-part process, which consists of awareness, clarification and recovery. Awareness has to do with getting enough perspective to observe our behavior pattern; clarification has to do with amplifying our understanding of the pattern; and recovery has to do with changing the pattern and finding a more balanced way to live.

Awareness

Many of us who are driven by compulsions are aware that we have no control over certain behaviors in our lives. We find ourselves at the mercy of erratic, powerful impulses, without knowing why—or what to do about them. Others of us experience only a vague sense of discomfort and anxiety; we may exhibit signs of psychological and/or physical distress. Often we *somatize* our discomfort; that is, we allow our bodies to act out our anxiety because it's too painful to face our distress consciously. If we don't know that we are acting compulsively, how do we wake up and see ourselves? And if we do realize or observe that a compulsive behavior has us by the scruff of the neck, how do we get more clarity about its destructive effect on our lives?

Many of us sleepwalk our way through either part or all of our lives—and then wonder why we stumble and fall. But fortunately, most of us will one day hear an ominous knocking at our psychological door that has come to wake us up. One form that knock can take is a compulsion—a warning signal that all is not well in our interior household. Perhaps we go on a spending spree that irreparably mutilates our budget, or maybe we floor the car's accelerator and wake up in the hospital. Perhaps our awakening is not so dramatic (and there is no guarantee that crises automatically create consciousness). Maybe a chance remark made by a co-worker or a loving confrontation by a close friend provides us with a mirror image of ourselves that we would not seek out. Or perhaps it is simply the goading of our own pain, our troubling sense that all is not well, that causes us to seek out a self-help group, to see an enlightening film, to find a helpful therapist or to pick up a book—perhaps a book like this one—that sheds a little light on the darkness we find ourselves in, that awakens a glimmer of awareness. There are as many ways to wake up as there are individuals to open their eyes.

This chapter will provide you with some background information for the trip you are about to take through a three-part process of self-discovery and change. It will share the true story of one woman who committed herself to the process, not knowing what she was in for—with life-changing results. And it will give you the opportunity to take a simple inventory that will enable you to get a clearer picture than you now have of the role of compulsive behaviors in your life. If you are squandering your valuable time, energy, money and resources on a self-defeating behavior, you need to know it! If you don't know you're doing it, you can't choose to change it.

After discovering the role of destructive mood-altering behaviors in your life, the second step in the process of awareness is learning to observe the cycle your negative behavior takes—what triggers it, how its energy builds to a crescendo, what happens in its aftermath. You can begin to watch for the internal hooks (thoughts and feelings) and the external ones (people, places and things) that act as instigators of your compulsive cycle.

Once you have learned to observe the cycle your compulsion follows, then you can track the pattern in which your cycle occurs. Does the cycle appear more frequently during times of stress? At holidays? When you are bored? When you are about to succeed at a difficult project? Finally, in this stage of the awareness process you can chart the destructive consequences of your cyclical pattern. You can observe and verify the correlation between your compulsive behavior and the aspects of your life that aren't working smoothly or are in total breakdown. Chapter Three will explain how to track your cycle and pattern.

As we saw in Chapter One, one function of mood-altering compulsions is to protect you from feeling painful emotions such as fear, shame and abandonment. As you arrive at a new perspective on your compulsivity by carefully cultivating awareness, the protective veil that kept you from experiencing your real feelings starts to lift, and you encounter your muffled emotions directly. Your wounded feelings are clues to the presence of unnamed, unknown, unmet needs, which usually originate in childhood. Chapter Four will explore your relationship to your feelings.

AN ILLUSTRATION: DANA'S STORY

Seeing the therapeutic process at work in someone else's life shows us the possibility of its working in ours. Dana's story, although it is more dramatic than most I have encountered, can teach us about the recovery process and about ourselves. Many compulsions are less intense than Dana's, but the more severe the childhood dysfunction, the more pervasive the subsequent mood-altering behavior.

Dana flounced into my office, her champagne-blonde hair tousled by the brisk January wind that had come up suddenly off the river. "Oh, Joan," she said, flashing me a dazzling smile, "you'll never guess what happened." Sauntering toward the low, leather-cushioned chair she usually sat in, Dana casually shed her full-length gray sheared mink coat, draping it carelessly over the back of the chair. The coat rested there precariously for a moment before falling to the floor in a heap. "I can hardly believe it," Dana continued animatedly, "but I've met the most wonderful man." She ran her long, manicured fingers through her hair, graced me with another brilliant smile and said coyly, "And see what he bought me?" Although I had become accustomed to seeing Dana as a walking jewelry display, I was taken aback by the obvious expense of her new diamond and sapphire drop earrings. Trying not to reveal a trace of astonishment, I said evenly, "They're lovely, Dana. Now tell me about your weekend."

In our four months of work together, I had repeatedly witnessed the glazed look in Dana's eyes that now prevented her from seeing what was so clear to me—the compulsive nature of her "relationships." Acting pleased about her exciting weekend, however, I listened attentively to the story of Dana's most recent flirtation with a marvelous man who had swept her off her feet with his good looks, money and charm, a man who had been looking all his life to settle down with the girl of his dreams.

Dana was riding the crest of a wave that would soon break, casting her onto a desolate beach where she would find only fragments of broken promises. At times like this I would seize the opportunity to ask a probing question or make a pointed comment that might elicit a glimmer of insight. Yet it was not until Dana passed into the downswing of her compulsive cycle that we could make any substantial progress. The rest of the time I acted as a stabilizing, calming presence, an advocate of the self Dana was in search of, a surrogate parent whose availability—unlike that of her own parents—was not governed by whim or caprice.

In the anticlimactic aftermath of one of her many seduction-based relationships, Dana would slowly start to recollect her shattered self-esteem. She would attend to a body that had been overly indulged with the finest foods and most sparkling wines at the most expensive restaurants, that had been a responsive plaything for a rich man indulging his fantasies. Dana would go to the gym to work out, she'd watch her weight, she'd tone and stretch and lift weights and eat giant salads.

But even as she was rebounding from one seductive episode, she was preparing for the next. Dana was readying herself for the hunt—the chase and the capture. Her dazzling, almond-eyed beauty was the tool of her seductive trade—and she knew how to hone it, refine it and use it to what she thought was her best advantage.

As Dana ricocheted off the downside of one seduction onto the upswing of the next, she intensified her preparations for the next conquest. A fabulous facial, a stunning new hairstyle, a smashing outfit from one of the best department stores—all became part of the high drama of seduction. Dressing up, creating the right character for a particular club was a way of molding, shaping and building to a crescendo the exciting process. Heading for an exclusive supper club, Dana would drive her little red sports car down the parkway, rock music blaring from the tape deck. She would begin to tremble from the excitement of the rush permeating her body; she felt as if she were hooked up to a giant generator sending power surges directly into her bloodstream. Part of the excitement was the exhilarating sense of power—the anticipation of the warrior about to make yet another conquest. But part of the sensation was fear—fear of loss of control or power in the game of seduction, where the stakes are high but there are no winners. Internally Dana was already out of control, in the grip of a behavior functioning autonomously, dragging her along in its wake.

DANA'S INCREASING AWARENESS

When Dana first came to me, she was suffering from a pain in the left side of her neck. Although her doctor could find no physiological basis for her pain, the dull but persistent ache continued to plague Dana until finally she was referred to me by a specialist who suggested that perhaps there was an emotional issue underlying her distress. It would not have occurred to Dana that the source of her pain was emotional. She was vaguely aware that something in her life was askew, but she could not have verbalized what it might be.

What Dana did tell me in our first encounter was that she was in the process of leaving an eighteen-month relationship with a millionaire who was providing for her, who had bought her a condominium in an exclusive suburb, who owned race cars and who had a private yacht on which he sometimes took her to Caribbean resorts. Although she enjoyed the benefits of second-hand wealth, Dana was growing tired of a relationship without a long-term commitment. Her lover's refusal to marry her and have a family was raising feelings of powerlessness and desperation in Dana, yet fear of giving up what she had was creating near-panic in her. There were screaming matches, broken china, hysteria, recrimination—and meanwhile Dana's biological clock was ticking as she approached her thirtieth birthday without children.

In the face of escalating tension, Dana did what most people with compulsions do—take action, any action. For her the accustomed action was her seduction ritual, which she used to reestablish her feelings of power and control. On the rebound from a fight with her lover and having taken refuge in an additional meaningless affair, Dana showed up in my office full of tension, guilt and tears. The first few months of our relationship were spent letting Dana talk, her rapid-fire phrases uttered staccato-style, like machine-gun fire. Her eyes moistening, she broke into fits of controlled crying. Heavy sobbing, which would have been therapeutic, was too dangerous; it would have meant giving up control of the deep feelings that were so threatening to Dana, the feelings she stifled by constantly taking refuge in her compulsive seductions.

My role in those early days was to provide a stable presence, an open space, a mirror in which Dana could gradually begin to perceive herself. As she told me her story and reflected on the behavior pattern that was becoming clearer and clearer in its retelling, she began to see that she managed her life by reaction. In the aftermath of a screaming match that usually propelled Dana to cruise the freeway for a seductive encounter to relieve her anxiety, she began to be able to postpone taking any drastic, chaotic action until she phoned me—or until she had an appointment. Then she could dump her fears in a safe place.

A week after Dana had excitedly recounted the details of her latest conquest, she sat across from me, dejected, teary-eyed, waiflike.

"What's going on?" I asked gently.

"It's been three days and I haven't heard from Arthur. I left four messages with his secretary yesterday, and last night I tried the apartment, but I can't reach him and he hasn't returned my calls."

The depth of Dana's despair was in poignant contrast to her jubilation of the week before. The need for constant reassurance that characterizes those of us with compulsions demands consistent feedback—phone calls, gifts, assurances of devotion.

"Why do you think you haven't heard from Arthur?" I probed.

I was not prepared for the flood of tears, the sobs, the incoherent words that followed.

"Dana, tell me how it feels not to hear from Arthur for three days."

"It feels like I'll never hear from him again; it feels like I'm all by myself on a glacier, like I'll never feel warm again."

"Do you remember ever feeling this way before?" I asked softly.

There was an uncharacteristic pause, a silence, while I just waited with Dana. The usual bubbly chatter, the gay laughter, the display of baubles, the "You'll never guess what happened, Joan" had been punctured. We were getting at the real feelings hidden beneath the counterfeit ones, the giddy highs and lows of Dana's seductive escapades. The emphasis on "he" that had dominated our hours together was giving way to the "me" whose story we needed to tell. Instead of "Oh Joan, I had to sleep until noon yesterday to recover from my exhausting weekend," it was "I'm freezing to death on a glacier—all by myself."

Dana's awareness began with her neck pain, continued with her increasing consciousness of her compulsive seduction pattern, and culminated in her deeply experiencing and naming feelings that had been hiding out for more than twenty years. Although at this stage of her therapeutic process she did not know where the feelings were coming from, what they indicated or what to do with them, she had encountered some powerful clues to be followed on the next lap of the road to recovery: clarification.

A REVIEW OF THE AWARENESS PROCESS

To review, by cultivating awareness you can do the following:

1. Learn to observe whether a compulsive, mood-altering behavior is negatively affecting your life.

2. Learn to observe and track the cycle and pattern of your compulsive behavior and chart its destructive consequences.

3. Learn to encounter the feelings that the compulsive behavior has been hiding.

Clarification

As a child experiencing emotional deprivation, whatever its form, you learned to compensate by creating, albeit unconsciously, a fantasy that made you feel safer, more secure, less powerless. Perhaps you learned to take care of other family members, denying your own needs, living inside the fantasy of powerful hero or self-sacrificing savior. Whatever the fantasy, it enabled you to order your experience and to survive the pain you felt—meanwhile subtly persuading you that there was no pain, no unmet need. You will learn more about identifying your particular unconscious fantasy in Chapter Five. Identifying your fantasy and clarifying its source also contributes to ever-increasing awareness, as it corroborates the insights you have already gained in your new perspective on your behavior pattern.

As we first noted in Chapter One, the fantasy we create in order to survive our early experiences is rooted in what may be termed "the family trance." This term describes the particular version of "reality" the family unit lives inside, a model that in some way serves the family system. The more dysfunctional the family system, the more each family member needs a fantasy to compensate for the pain and the more likely it is that a compulsive behavior will develop. By reconstructing the family trance and the role you played in it as a child, you can, from your adult vantage point, put together the pieces of the puzzle in a way that helps you see a cause-and-effect relationship in your life. As we saw in our discussion of compulsive behavior patterns, we can change only what we see—not what we are oblivious to. We can't change our fantasy and the role we adopted in our family trance unless we are conscious of them and develop some perspective on them. Chapter Six will explain how to recognize the family trance and break its spell.

Once the spell has been broken and the family trance has been revealed, you can clearly see the role that both your unconscious fantasy and your compulsive behavior pattern have played in protecting you from feelings you might not have been able to withstand as a child. But as an adult, with resources you did not have as a child, you can decide to trade in illusion for reality. You can face your painful feelings, your deprivation, your role in the family trance—and the compulsive behavior they spawned. You have a choice you did not have before: You can continue to act in the family play, or you can unmask, write a new script and wear your own face. But you cannot move forward until you mourn the loss of the fantasy, your lifelong companion that protected you from reality at the cost of your true self. Adapting some rituals from Chapter Seven to your own life story will help you move from old illusions to new realities.

DANA'S CLARIFICATION PROCESS

Dana's experiences in her clarification process can help us with our own.

After Dana's first wrenching acknowledgment that she was feeling as if she were freezing to death on a glacier, I began to help her piece together the scraps and bits she haltingly, painfully started to give me about her past. The crazy quilt that temporarily emerged was eventually supplanted by a pattern with order and meaning—however painful it was to see that pattern. Behind the facade of Dana's "normal," middle-class family lay a nightmare of alcoholism, sexual abuse, secrecy and manipulation. The most compromising of clandestine bargains was struck in the interests of "preserving the family." One of the most insidious was Dana's tacit consent never to tell about her father's drunken secret midnight visits to her attic bedroom—consent she was forced to give due to her terror of her violent father, in exchange for which he made her his "little princess." What was too painful for Dana to realize was that this bargain demanded that she give up the deepest part of her being to fill a role forced upon her by someone else's need and desire. With no family member who could be trusted, and eventually no self who could be trusted either, Dana lived in a perpetual state of emotional abandonment. She learned to identify with the role she had learned for survival, a role made tolerable only by the rewards she accrued for a fine performance.

Dana began to see why she felt she was freezing to death on a glacier. Growing up in an abusive family means that we never have the sense of trust we need to tide us over the rough spots, the emotional lows we all have. Dana's ongoing emotional entanglement with her family of origin ensured that, until the disastrous knots had been internally untied, she would forever feel powerless. Until she had journeyed inwardly to the source of her distress, she would be doomed to repeat the seductive pattern that she had been forced to learn at an early age—a pattern that had unconsciously become the compulsion that governed her life.

Compulsive behavior patterns take root in a situation that is abusive to the self at a person's core. For the compulsion to come to full flower, it needs to be cultivated in the soil of an unconscious fantasy. A child suffering abuse in a family where there is no hope of respite or rescue learns to find solace in the fantasy. The fantasy may be that a fairy godmother will appear to whisk the child away, but whatever it is, it is not grounded in reality. Yet it does provide the child with the illusion that life is bearable, orderly and manageable—in an unbearable, disorderly and unmanageable situation. The construction of this fantasy allows the child to go on living in a dysfunctional environment without feeling that death is imminent. By the time the child becomes an adult, the fantasy has become so integral to living that it effectively masquerades as reality.

A child needs the solace of a fantasy. It is crucial for an adult to understand how smart it was to construct a fantasy as a shelter to hide out in. But the next step is to see that, as an adult, one has resources that were never available to the child and that the adult can appropriate those resources.

The next step for Dana was the realization that she had built a fantasy as a protection—that she had reached out a million times in the past to other human beings and it had not worked, but the fantasy had always worked; it was always available to her. And then she needed to name the fantasy, give it up and, finally, mourn it.

For Dana, the seduction compulsion was grounded in the fantasy of the knight in shining armor who would reward her for her sexual sizzle with his power, his money, his influence, his protection. Because the illusion had worked so bountifully, bringing her everything that money could buy, she could still nourish the belief that she could always command someone to be emotionally available—provided that she knew the commodity of exchange. The unconscious belief system this fantasy fostered was that only men could take care of her. Other women were of little importance in her life (after all, her mother had not protected her), and Dana certainly did not feel competent to take care of herself. Thus the panic when she did not hear from her latest lover for three days; thus the dependency on a powerful man to protect her against the vicissitudes of life, against being alone in the world, against her abusive family.

Eventually Dana came to see that her fantasy, conceived in the family trance, was a betrayal. Then she could begin to ask hard, reality-bound questions: "Why wasn't Arthur home for three days?" "Who was that woman who answered John's phone?"

Watching the dismantling of her fantasy, Dana felt once again the feelings of rage and powerlessness, of abandonment and emptiness that she had felt so long ago as a child in the breeding grounds of her seduction compulsion. But as her awareness increased, as she began to trust her own perceptions, she began to be able to take baby steps toward emotional health. One of the first concrete actions she was able to manage was not to give her phone number to a man she met one evening at a restaurant. Taking this small step, she found herself assailed by feelings of terror and desperation. She felt if she did not go out with this man, no one else would turn up. But she held fast, aware of her feelings but not giving in to them. Later she would get the payoff; she would feel stronger, less dependent, more autonomous. Each simple step built on the previous one. But, in the beginning, it was blind faith and my emotional support that enabled her to make a small change in her lifelong behavior pattern.

As the fantasy began to die its own death, I encouraged Dana to cry, to make up a burial ritual for the person who had embraced that fantasy, to do some role-playing so that the death could be personified. I asked her to imagine that she saw the fantasy in front of her, like a photograph, and to actually speak out loud to it and express her feelings of mourning. Of course it was inevitable that Dana would be angry about this death too—angry especially with me, who had acted as executioner's assistant.

As Dana began to be willing to sacrifice her mood-altering experiences for reality, as she finally connected her compulsive behavior to her pain, she was able to reassess her former relationships. She was able to say, "I've got to stay out of this situation because the chances are that it is not good for me and I'll be hurt again." But for every bit of progress, for every time she didn't give out her phone number, there were some slips backward.

Through her clarification process, Dana was able to discover, name and give up the fantasy that had ruled her life for so long. Understanding and reexperiencing her family trance through unearthed feelings enabled Dana to see the cause-and-effect principle at work in her life. She was able to exchange illusion for reality, coming face to face with the empowering realization that she had a choice she had never seen before—she didn't have to be daddy's "little princess" any more.

A REVIEW OF THE CLARIFICATION PROCESS

To review, through the clarification process we can do the following:

1. Learn to identify and name our unconscious fantasy.

2. Learn to uncover our family trance and the role we played in it.

3. Learn to exchange illusion for reality, mourning the death of our lifelong fantasy.

Recovery

Before you can replace destructive old patterns with healthy new ones, you must take an inventory of your needs. What must you have in your life—physically, emotionally and spiritually—to live in a balanced, creative way? Remembering that a compulsion represents a misguided attempt to compensate for some radical imbalance, you come to see that your best protection against slipping back into old behavior patterns—or creating unhealthy new ones—is to find fulfilling alternatives to the old, accustomed ways of behaving. Chapter Eight offers assessment guidelines so that you can learn to formulate new responses to perpetual needs.

Having taken a realistic needs inventory, you can then, in Chapters Nine and Ten, consciously begin to plan life patterns that provide nourishment to your whole being. You will need to do the following:

1. Cultivate your sense of spontaneity and playfulness.

2. Bring balance to your life, especially by learning relaxation techniques such as exercises for breathing and perhaps meditation.

3. Learn to behave less impulsively by overcoming your immature emotions.

4. Work on learning to say no to hurtful experiences and to set realistic goals.

5. Cultivate trust in your own perceptions rather than relying on others for the truth.

6. Learn to experience life's "natural highs" rather than seeking compulsive or substance-induced mood alterations.

7. Learn to replace the excitement of compulsion-spawned crises with serenity.

All the awareness and self-help techniques in the world won't work unless you build a support system as a foundation for personal change and growth. Any realistic recovery plan recognizes the need for relationships with trusted individuals and may include a support group, a competent therapist, a twelve-step program and what the "anonymous" programs (such as Alcoholics Anonymous, Gamblers Anonymous, etc.) refer to as a *Higher Power.* Through the external emotional support that these relationships provide, you will learn to gradually build that support within yourself. Only the external touchstone that these relationships provide can powerfully support you and call you to account as you continue to travel the road to recovery. You will learn how to build a strong support system in Chapter Ten.

DANA'S RECOVERY

Dana's growth did not prevent her from making a number of "slips" — that is, reverting to old compulsive behaviors. Such slips are incredibly important, for they tell us how we are doing. They are yardsticks, demarcation lines, and they help us move into deeper and deeper levels of awareness and clarification on our road to recovery. During this time Dana would come in and tell me about someone she'd met, how she'd indicated her availability and how he'd responded. "I know I'm in fantasy," she'd say, "but I've got to do it anyway." Such incidents have to be repeated many times; they help you do the life research you need if you are to clarify and test your newly born awareness by learning to accept and express emotions. At such times you can help yourself by accepting the slips you've made and knowing that they are part of your natural growth out of the fantasy that has possessed you into the reality that beckons you.

About eight months into Dana's recovery, she met a man who was much younger than she was. Although it seemed that this relationship could never be long-term for a number of reasons, I encouraged Dana in it because it represented such a divergence from her usual pattern. This kind, gentle young man, who was dazzled by Dana, was able to nurture a side of her that no one else had ever touched. The vulnerable, insecure, deeply loving person underneath her sizzlingly sexy exterior was able to feel safe with this young man. "I love him because he has a pure heart," she would say. Because he was a financially strapped art student on scholarship, he could never offer Dana the trappings of the sophisticated life she was used to. Such a change was healthy for her and showed her another way to be in a relationship.

Subsequent to this relationship, further along in her recovery, Dana was able to make a commitment that would have been unthinkable the year before—not to date anyone for a few months. Although she balked at my suggestion, Dana eventually realized that, given her history, the only way she could develop a strong sense of autonomy and independence was by staying away from the dating scene altogether for a while. Later on, when she had shored up her own energy and security sufficiently, she could return to the couples world with a different attitude.

It was during this period that Dana turned to a variety of strategies that enabled her to work toward meeting her own needs, freeing her from the enslaving compulsion that had ruled her life. She was responsive to my suggestion that she keep a journal. Writing her story helped her take the long view of where she'd come from and where she was going. She began to notice, almost as if from outside herself, her feelings when she was with a man. She participated in several psychodrama workshops, acting out some of her inner dramas, helping them come to life. Every time she got the urge to cruise the expressway or go to a nightclub, she called either me or one of ten people whose names she had on a phone list she kept on her refrigerator. She regularly attended Al-Anon meetings to deal with the issues from her family of origin. She worked off excess energy at the local gym. And somewhere along the way her mysterious neck pain disappeared altogether.

Because she had never learned to take care of herself emotionally, I suggested that Dana consciously cultivate caretaking by buying herself a doll. She was to notice how she took care of this surrogate child—whether she discarded it underneath the bed, whether she left it unattended for days or whether she fed it, clothed it, nurtured it, sang to it. She was to give this doll all the emotional attention she had never received as a child. After a period of neglecting the doll, Dana learned to shower upon it all the loving attention she herself had craved but been deprived of.

But the most visible task that Dana worked on was the creation of her own business. Although it felt to her like pulling teeth, she stuck to the monotonous, unrewarding tasks of goal-setting, getting professional training, making lists, obtaining a small business loan, locating an office site and setting up shop. Although it took two years, Dana stuck to her plan, despite her many temptations to return to her old lifestyle of shopping and manicures. But finally, with a well-deserved sense of accomplishment, Dana opened an export/import business. And when she had survived her period of celibacy, she returned to the world of men with a new self-confidence.

All Dana's hard work paid off. Her business became hugely successful, and she now has a husband who is her equal, not her protector, and two children. Although Dana is no longer my client, she still keeps in touch. Now when I hear her lilting voice on the other end of the phone saying "Oh, Joan, you won't believe what happened!" I know it's not the voice of illusion speaking.

By discovering what her real needs were, Dana could take steps to meet them. She began to take responsibility for her behavior—to notice when she was feeling afraid and use well-developed strategies to feel more secure; to set limits with friends and family members and particularly with men; to set goals, which enabled her to start her own business and become financially self-supporting; and to cultivate serenity rather than seduction-induced highs. Dana also worked hard to build a foundation of supportive relationships. Her Al-Anon program, her phone list of supportive group members, her friends and her loving relationship with her new family were all part of the firm base she created for her new, compulsion-free life.

A REVIEW OF THE RECOVERY PROCESS

To review, in recovery you can accomplish the following:

1. Learn to assess your physical, emotional and spiritual needs.

2. Learn to create healthy life patterns, bringing balance and serenity to your everyday routine.

3. Learn to build a strong support system of healthy relationships as the basis of your new, compulsion-free life.

Taking Inventory

You may not be a movie binger like Harry, a haircutter like Monica, a charge account devotee like Vanessa or a perpetual seductress like Dana. You may be driven by a less obvious and socially approved behavior pattern such as exercising, working or winning. Perhaps you have a secret compulsive behavior—such as eyebrow tweezing or calling people on the telephone and hanging up—that you haven't admitted could possibly be destructive to your life. Or maybe you have a universally recognized problem such as gambling.

All of us engage in mood-altering behaviors. If we are bored, we may turn on the television; if we are mentally overstimulated, we may play soft music or escape into a murder mystery. Mood alteration is part of being human—if we choose it and if it doesn't interfere with our lives. When we don't consciously choose it, however, and when it is interfering with our lives, then it signals that our behavior may be compulsive. A compulsion feels irresistible, impulsive, even irrational. You feel that you *have* to do something, that you've been nudged or even catapulted into a behavior that you didn't consciously choose. And you feel compelled to repeat the behavior, perhaps frequently or perhaps only occasionally.

The following inventory is designed to help you discover whether, and to what extent, a compulsive behavior is running your life.

QUESTIONNAIRE: IS A COMPULSION RUNNING YOUR LIFE?

Part I

1. Do you frequently feel driven to engage in a particular mood-altering behavior?

2. Do you often fantasize about engaging in a particular mood-altering behavior?

3. Do you feel ashamed of or embarrassed by a particular mood-altering behavior?

4. Do you habitually hide a mood-altering behavior from your family, friends or co-workers?

5. Does a mood-altering behavior affect your social standing or reputation?

6. Does a mood-altering behavior interfere with your family life or your primary relationship?

7. Does a mood-altering behavior consistently cause you to miss work or be late for work?

8. Does a mood-altering behavior frequently cause you to disregard the feelings of others?

9. Are episodes of a mood-altering behavior occurring more frequently?

10. Do you usually engage in a mood-altering behavior after a setback, a letdown or an argument?

11. Do you consistently arrange circumstances so that you can engage in a particular mood-altering behavior?

12. Do you spend time trying to talk yourself out of engaging in a mood-altering behavior?

13. Do you consistently lie about engaging in a mood-altering behavior?

14. Do you often engage in a particular mood-altering behavior because you feel depressed, anxious or bored?

15. Do you avoid thinking abut the consequences of a particular mood-altering behavior?

16. Do you feel increased tension, anxiety or depression when you refrain from engaging in a mood-altering behavior?

17. Do you seek out people you have nothing in common with to engage in a mood-altering behavior?

18. Do you often feel that, if you were happier, you wouldn't need a particular mood-altering behavior?

19. Do you cultivate certain friends for the purpose of engaging in a particular mood-altering behavior?

20. Does a mood-altering behavior endanger your physical safety or well-being—or the safety of others?

21. Do you become defensive or angry when confronted about a particular mood-altering behavior?

22. Do you sometimes consider seeing a helping professional or attending a self-help group because of a mood-altering behavior?

If you answered "yes" to four or more of the above questions, your response is a warning signal that a destructive, mood-altering behavior may be running your life.

Part II

1. Do you often wish that you could stop yourself from engaging in a particular mood-altering behavior?

2. After engaging in a particular mood-altering behavior, do you find you can't wait to do it again?

3. Do your family, friends or co-workers make comments about your mood-altering behavior?

4. Do you consistently jeopardize your budget in order to spend more money on a mood-altering behavior?

5. Does a mood-altering behavior consistently interfere with your ability to set goals or accomplish tasks?

6. Do occurrences of a mood-altering behavior cause you to break the law?

7. Do you frequently feel a lowered sense of self-esteem after engaging in a particular mood-altering behavior?

8. Do you violate your own value system to engage in a mood-altering behavior?

If you answered "yes" to one or more of the questions in Part II of this questionnaire, your response strongly indicates that a destructive mood-altering behavior may be running your life. Although it will take effort and commitment, you—like the men and women whose stories appear in these pages—can overcome the compulsive behaviors that interfere with your life. By following the steps and doing the exercises that are provided in the following chapters, you can find the balance and serenity that so many of my clients have found.

CHAPTER THREE

Tracking
Your Compulsive Pattern
and Its Consequences

A former client of mine who frequently travels to Europe on business reported this incident. He had taken an overnight flight from New York to Paris and arrived at his hotel, tired and irritated, hoping for a few hours of sleep before his afternoon meeting. The bellboy showed him to a lovely room on the fourteenth floor, set down his bags and thanked him for a generous tip.

Casting an appreciative glance at the freshly made double bed, the executive heaved a sigh of relief at the prospect of a few hours of real sleep in a real bed. Just as he drew back the covers and started to settle into the silence of the room, the businessman overheard a few bars of some hearty French bistro music. Thinking that perhaps the maid had left the radio or TV on, he checked the dials and convinced himself the music had floated up from the street. Climbing back into bed, he started to settle down, and then he once again heard a lilting refrain that would have been a welcome sound at any time except 9:00 a.m.

Now thoroughly annoyed and convinced that the music was in the next room, the sleepy executive called the reception desk and demanded a room on a different floor. The bellboy reappeared and showed the American to a room on the twelfth floor, directly beneath his previous room. Gratefully, the businessman once again cast longing glances at the bed that promised a few hours of uninterrupted sleep. Again tipping the bellboy and turning down the covers, the executive sank onto the mattress. His head had just hit the pillow when a few strains of the same music caught his ear. Outraged and exhausted, the businessman again called the desk, demanding a room on the other side of the hotel. Grumbling under his breath, the man was shown to a small, dark room towards the back of the hotel. As the bellboy set down the bags and switched on the lights, a look of slight amusement swept across his face. Once again the light, tinkling sounds of bistro music invaded the room. Kneeling down beside the suitcases, the bellboy glued his ear to a small flight bag. "Monsieur," he said with a devilish twinkle in his eye, "la radio!" Sheepishly, the American ferreted out a small transistor radio from among the bag's contents. Sure enough, he had left the radio on. Neither room 1409 nor room 1209 nor other hotel guests nor street musicians were the culprits; the executive himself had caused his own discomfort.

◇◇◇

My client didn't need me to point out to him the obvious: that we create many of our own problems by the programs—radio or otherwise—that we carry with us and that when we change the station or flick the off switch, we can alter and improve the quality of our lives. Craziness has been defined as repeating the same behavior pattern while expecting a different outcome. Certainly many people with compulsive behavior patterns continuously repeat those destructive patterns, not understanding that until they change internally, their external circumstances will remain the same.

Tracking the Pattern
of a Compulsive Rescuer

One of the most insidious compulsions I have encountered is *rescuing,* also known as *caretaking.* Because it is so common and so culturally acceptable, it is not perceived to be as destructive as more obvious, less acceptable compulsions such as gambling, spending, speeding, seduction and crisis creation. Nevertheless, rescuing is insidious precisely because it is highly rewarded and because it is so pervasive in the rescuer's personality that it frequently goes undetected. Compulsive rescuers may feel only a sense of general discomfort, a troubling sense that life is not living up to its promise, that there should be more than they're experiencing.

JOANNE'S STORY

Joanne was a bright, energetic young woman in her early thirties. Goaded into therapy by the relentless ticking of her biological clock, Joanne was afraid that, if all her relationships ended up as the previous three had, she would never marry and become a mother. Oblivious to the fact that she was already mothering a ready-made family—a father, a mother and a younger brother—Joanne had no idea when she arrived in my office that she was a compulsive rescuer. All she knew was that she was having difficulty maintaining a committed relationship, and she had no idea why. As a child, Joanne had contributed to the family finances by turning over a good portion of her babysitting earnings. Then she had put herself through college and gotten a good job as a journalist on a daily newspaper with a circulation of 50,000. Her success in the marketplace was in a distinct contrast to her family's failure, but Joanne's productivity only intensified her belief that her competence was a matter of luck that somehow made her even more responsible for her family's welfare.

Because Joanne's brother, Johnny, had not graduated from high school, the only job he could get was as a short-order cook. An unskilled laborer plagued with health problems, Joanne's father had a part-time position as a night watchman, a job he frequently missed because his arthritis was kicking up, his high blood pressure was out of control or Johnny's car (which served as transportation for Johnny and his father) had broken down and there was no way for him to get to work. Johnny himself had had several car accidents in the last four years, and his insurance policy was precarious—as was his temper, which got him into scrapes at work and had even cost him a couple jobs.

Joanne's mother, Harriet, who made feeble attempts to keep the family from disintegrating, was a wisp of a woman who spent a good deal of time crying, wringing her hands and calling Joanne long distance. "I don't want to drag you into this," Harriet would begin when Joanne asked how things were at home. "You've been so nice to us already; I don't want you to be involved." Harriet's "reluctance" to communicate only intensified Joanne's concern.

"What is it?" Joanne would plead. "What's happened?"

"Well, Papa had a coughing fit yesterday."

"Don't you think he should go to the doctor?"

"Well, yes, but we couldn't get him there the last time we made an appointment because the brakes on Johnny's car weren't working."

Inevitably Joanne would end up sending money not only for Papa's doctor bill, but also for Johnny's brakes. And inevitably, too, this kind of incident would repeat itself over and over again. Within approximately three years, Joanne had "loaned" over $12,000 to her unfortunate family.

The year that Joanne began therapy, she had been unable to go on vacation because a sudden costly family emergency had made it impossible for her to pay her airfare to Greece. She had rescheduled the trip, which she was going to take with a friend, for the coming August and was eagerly marking off the weeks until her departure. One Wednesday, the usual day for Joanne's appointment, I noticed an unusual air of resignation in Joanne's bearing and a lackluster look in her eye.

"Joanne," I approached cautiously, "how are you feeling today?"

"I'm feeling really upset," she responded with a note of sadness in her voice.

"Oh," I probed, "did something happen?"

"Well, I'm feeling really disappointed," Joanne continued. "I'm not going to be able to go on vacation this year after all. It appears that Papa is going to have to undergo surgery, and there are going to be a lot of extra bills. We may have to hire someone to stay with him after he comes home from the hospital."

"Can't your mother or Johnny stay with him sometimes?" I continued.

"Mother is too upset, and I can't count on Johnny. But it seems so unfair that I don't get to go on vacation for two years in a row. My friend Marge's mother had surgery last year and she went on vacation; why can't I?"

As we explored Joanne's feelings further, it became clear that she saw no choices in this dilemma. If she was a dutiful daughter—as she was—then she had to stay home to save money for her family. Being available to parents is what dutiful daughters did. It was that simple. It did seem strange to Joanne, she said, that as a child she had missed out on so many good times—and that, even though she had worked hard and been responsible, Fate had once again arranged it so that she was missing out on good times as an adult. If that were her lot in life, however, she would just have to accept it.

In the wake of exploring Joanne's feelings about missing her vacation, Joanne and I had the opportunity to look at other feelings she had never before expressed. It was only through the pain of realizing that yet another year was going by and she wasn't getting any time off that Joanne began probing more deeply. One Wednesday Joanne mentioned that her mother had called her the previous Sunday morning. "Oh," I said casually, "how are things going with the family?"

"Well, my mother needs dental work," said Joanne. "I'll have to send her some money."

"I'm sorry to hear that. Joanne, let me ask you something. How did you feel after your mother's phone call?"

"Interesting that you should ask that, because I found myself going back to bed at noon, and I had made plans to go jogging with friends. I just didn't seem to have my usual energy."

"So you didn't get to go jogging with your friends?"

"No, I ended up taking a nap and watching some television."

"Joanne, have you noticed how many times lately you haven't gotten to do something that you planned to do? You're going to miss your vacation in August, you've missed a couple of lunches and dinners with friends and now you've even missed jogging on a Sunday afternoon."

I could see a little light go on behind Joanne's eyes. As we started to work on this issue more deeply, Joanne began to admit into consciousness her feelings about her mother's phone calls. She began to notice that the Sunday phone ritual left her somewhat depressed, unenergetic, unfocused. She reported that lately she felt as if she were drifting around her apartment in an uncharacteristic stupor, as if she were waiting for something. She really didn't understand why she felt depressed after talking to her mother; she *loved* to talk to her mother, she said.

JOANNE'S COMPULSIVE PATTERN

I suggested that Joanne keep a large piece of lined paper taped to the table next to the phone so that she could record a key sentence or two from her mother's phone conversations. After the interchange, Joanne was to write down what she said in response to key sentences and also to record her feelings at the end of the conversation. What we discovered was that invariably

Joanne's mother would say something like, "I'm so worried about your father." Joanne's response was likely to be a variation of "What's the matter? Is something wrong?"

Trigger to Action

As we noted in Chapter One, every compulsive behavior cycle begins with what can be called the "trigger to action." As we shall see in this chapter, the trigger can be an internal one or an external one, depending on the person, the compulsion and the circumstances. External triggers include people, places and things. Clearly, all behavior results from an interior motivation. What we are differentiating here, though, is whether a person, place or thing in the outside world sets off a usually dormant thought or feeling or whether the trigger is purely internal, unprovoked by an external stimulus. By locating the trigger that indicates the onset of a compulsive behavior cycle, by concretely observing it and labeling it, we can make choices about alternative ways to deal with it, respond to it and manage it.

By asking Joanne to listen for and then to write down key statements that her mother made, I was helping her to become aware of the onset of her compulsive behavior cycle. We discovered that when her mother said, "I'm so worried about your father," and then paused, with a meaning-filled hesitation, Joanne's pulse quickened, she began to feel anxious and she started to question her mother, who initially hesitated and appeared unwilling to give any additional information. But the hidden agenda here, apparently unconscious in both parties, was that the mother was inviting her daughter's questions without being willing to say so.

The hesitation was the clue to the daughter that things at home were not really going well, and the unconscious expectation on the mother's part was that the daughter would step in and say, "What happened?" After another hesitation, the mother would say resignedly, "Well, nothing happened; I don't want to upset you." Of course this statement was another clue to what was happening underneath the surface. If the mother indicated that the daughter might be upset by what she had to communicate, then something upsetting was certainly going on.

At this point Joanne, whose anxiety was escalating, was likely to plead, "Tell me. Please tell me." Although the mother appeared not to be seeking help, she was giving strong signals that she *did* want help. Because the daughter loved the mother and the mother appeared to be helpless and needy, she wanted to be helpful and fell right into the ensnaring net—which meant that she'd have to pay more money or solve more problems that the family seemed incapable of solving themselves.

Response

As soon as Joanne began to watch this interaction almost as if it were happening to someone other than herself, she became aware of the internal tailspin initiated by the external trigger. "I'm worried about your father," an outer, verbal stimulus, was such a powerful statement that it provoked anxiety, caused a variety of bodily reactions (including fear for her family's well-being, a pounding heart and sweaty palms) and elicited the desired response—offers of money or other aid. When Joanne made her offer of assistance, her feeling of fear was replaced by a feeling of power. She had saved her family again!

Other feelings and thoughts this powerful trigger statement evoked in Joanne included a sense of responsibility for her family's plight, guilt that she was in better financial circumstances than they and a sense of dutiful obligation to make it all better for her unfortunate parents and impulsive brother.

The actual cycle this trigger statement would set off varied in length and intensity according to the severity of the circumstances. After a phone call indicating her family's financial need, Joanne would typically feel afraid that some harm would befall her family. Then she would feel an upsurge of energy, an impetus toward activity that could "save" her family. She would set about checking her bank balances and seeing how much money was available to be wired to her parents' account. If there was a problem because Johnny's car insurance had been cancelled, she would start making phone calls to agents and insurance companies—since no other family member seemed to know how to proceed.

Depending on the nature of the emergency she was saving everyone from, Joanne's compulsive rescuing process could last a few hours or a few days. When Papa had finally had a checkup, Mother had paid the mortgage and Johnny had obtained a new insurance policy, Joanne felt a cathartic sense of relief and a surge of powerful satisfaction at having rescued her family from the brink of disaster. She could bask in the glow of appreciation from her grateful, beleaguered mother, who hated to ask her much-loved daughter for assistance when she had given so much already. Joanne could feel good about having lived up to her role as a dutiful daughter. She felt empathic, powerful, caring.

It was only a week or so later, when Joanne sat down with her own budget and her own proposed vacation plans, that she would discover, with a sinking feeling, that the extent of the financial damage was greater than she had realized—that, having paid for the mortgage, the insurance premium, the doctor's bill, the new brakes on Johnny's car, she was left with a minimum of resources herself. At these times Joanne would go into a tailspin and resolve to see if she could find some other way of helping her family without resorting to her own pocketbook.

Because the trigger that initiated Joanne's rescuing compulsion was an external one—that is, a particular person who called for help—Joanne's compulsive behavior cycle was governed from outside herself. Her rescuing was a knee-jerk response to her mother's phone calls, particularly to such statements as "I'm worried about your father." The cycle itself usually lasted anywhere from a day to a week, depending on the severity of the family predicament.

Increasing Awareness

The pattern the cycle took—that is, how frequently the rescuing incidents occurred and at what times of year—began to emerge as Joanne started keeping track of her mother's phone calls, the trigger statements and the ensuing cyclical rescuing behavior. The desperate phone calls seemed to escalate around holidays and vacations—times when families frequently experience mounting tensions as their expectations collide with reality.

Joanne noticed, for example, that Thanksgiving induced a particularly heavy-duty rescue effort on her part. She realized that, despite year after year of the same futile expectations, the same dashed hopes, she always expected an idyllic holiday scene. She would look forward to being with her family for a celebrative holiday, but what happened was that she would end up doing the shopping, she would find herself doing all the cooking and it would be left to her to manage the other festive preparations—virtually alone. More draining than any physical preparations, however, were the emotional responsibilities she assumed. She found herself making seemingly endless numbers of calls to coordinate who was coming for dinner, when they would arrive, where they would stay and how they would get along with Johnny, whose unpredictable temperament kept everyone on tenterhooks.

As Joanne watched the family drama unfold, she could see that she was pursuing an illusion that was unattached to reality. Because she longed to have a caring family, it was crucial that she create one—even though each family member was screaming loud and clear (if nonverbally) that she was *not* cared for. The fantasy of sitting down to Thanksgiving dinner, of being together, had so dominated her expectations that she had been willing to overlook the reality that was staring her in the face. The unconscious thought that shaped her compulsive rescuing behavior was "If I don't orchestrate a family dinner, I won't have a family." The thought that drove her compulsion was that she must create Thanksgiving—or else there would be no family. The feeling directly resulting from the thought "I won't have a family" was "I will be totally lost." To admit that feeling into consciousness would have been too terrifying for Joanne; thus the frenzied, constant rescuing of this disconnected family was a concerted effort to avoid knowing that there was no caring family—to avoid the experience of feeling lost.

As is always the case, Joanne's outer life was a reflection of her inner attitudes and beliefs—despite her unconscious illusions to the contrary. Although she was an active person with many friends who loved tennis and water skiing, volleyball and bonfires on the beach, Joanne did not seem able to sustain any intimate relationships (which, of course, brought her into my office for therapy). As we noted in Chapter One, if we carefully follow the clues in a person's story, they will always lead us to the reason for their discomfort.

The reason in Joanne's case, which was apparent to others but not to her, was that the repository of Joanne's emotional life was her family. In any situation involving deep feelings, she reverted to her role in the family—that of rescuer. Since she already had "children" in the form of her parents and younger brother, there was no room for a nuclear family of her own. Her energy was so used up perpetuating her illusion that she had none left for intimate relationships of her own. Finally the depression and fatigue she felt after her mother's Sunday phone calls began to slip through the cracks of her iron-tight rescuer cover. As she and I worked on what troubled her, Joanne discovered that she loved the fantasy of having a mother—and that her unconscious belief was that she was powerful enough to force Harriet, the woman who had given birth to her, to be the mother she wanted. Somewhere deep in her being she believed she had the capacity to force all these people to be the family she longed for—even though they had been shouting "no," even though they had been taking her money and ruining her vacation plans for years.

Preparing to Change

When Joanne became comfortable with the idea that her recent feelings of depression after her mother's calls were totally normal (considering the recurring unconscious dynamic she was locked into) and, in fact, predictable, when she realized that she was bound to feel this way as she uncovered the illusion she had staked her life on, she was willing to engage in an exercise designed to bring more awareness and pave the way for healthy changes.

On the lined paper Joanne was keeping next to the phone, I asked her to continue to record the trigger statements her mother made each week—and to begin gradually to change her responses to them. After identifying certain phrases that were almost irresistible, that virtually guaranteed the instantaneous triggering of compulsive rescuing, Joanne could move from knee-jerk responses to considered, deliberate answers. "I don't want to upset you," "I'm worried about your father" and "I know you've got your own life" all produced immediate emotional reactions in Joanne.

"I know you've got your own life" was particularly terrifying because it preyed on her fear that without a family, she was lost. To be separated, to have her own life—distant and removed from mother, father and brother— was to insinuate that her parents and sibling were all together as a unit and that she was outside, all by herself, emotionally alone. The tragic but well-guarded secret fact was, of course, that she *was* alone emotionally—despite her illusion to the contrary—and the sooner she could see reality without the overlay she had constantly imposed upon it, the greater the claim she could lay to leading her own unencumbered life.

Changing the Response

As part of Joanne's growth process, she created, with my help, a list of alternative responses she could give to her mother's trigger statements—as well as a list of "neutral" or "interesting" topics that Joanne could introduce as a way out of concentrating on the usual subjects of family disaster. Let's examine some of the various responses Joanne used as a way of avoiding her usual knee-jerk compulsive reactions to her mother's trigger statements.

"I'm really worried about your father," Joanne's mother might begin. Early in her recovery Joanne might choose the response "Yes, I'm worried about Daddy, too." Although such a response would acknowledge her mother's concern about her father's health and would express Joanne's own concern, it would allow her to avoid the old impulse to jump in and rescue her mother. Previously Joanne might have said nervously, "Why? What's the matter? Is something wrong?" Although this simple statement might seem easy for most people to make, it was difficult for Joanne because the feelings that came up for her were feelings of guilt—feelings that she was a bad person for not rushing in to make the situation all better. There are profound repercussions to changing behaviors that are twenty-five or thirty years old. But because Joanne and I had prepared for this interaction with her mother and because Joanne didn't have to think up this new response on the spot, she was able to avoid starting the compulsive rescuing syndrome.

A response Joanne might use a little further along in her recovery to answer her mother's "I'm worried about your father" might be "I hope he's taking his medicine the way the doctor told him to." This response, a bit more distant than "I'm worried, too," would acknowledge her father's condition, her mother's concern and Joanne's empathy and compassion—without Joanne's being as emotionally involved as she had been in her previous response. Although Joanne's strength and clarity were growing, she found it difficult, just as she had at the beginning of her recovery, to answer her mother's desperation-clad pleas with her new detachment. What surfaced when Joanne made this statement were powerful feelings of fear—fear for her mother, whom she felt she was abandoning in the midst of a crisis, and fear for herself in the impending emotional isolation she dreaded if she were cut adrift from her family.

Getting Stronger

Joanne held fast to her resolve to exchange illusion for reality; eventually, as she grew stronger in her way of relating to her mother, she could actually bring herself, with some effort, to make a previously unthinkable response to "I'm worried about your father." "Uh huh," she said in acknowledgement. Then, "Gee, Mom, did you know that I'm going to get another promotion?"

This response made Joanne feel absolutely uncompassionate, like a "bad" daughter, but as she persevered in her alternative statements, she noticed her post-phone-call depression slipping away and her energy level rising, bit by bit. Her list of appropriate phone topics gave her a wealth of things to talk to her mother about—from her friend Janet's new baby to the game show host who was scheduled to be the commencement speaker at Joanne's alma mater. The goal was for Joanne to talk about herself, prompting her mother to meet some of Joanne's needs for a change.

As a result of her highly motivated intervention in her compulsive behavior pattern, Joanne came to a clear-eyed view of the destructive consequences of her rescuing cycles. She discovered, to her dismay, that she had permanently parted with thousands of dollars; had missed vacations for two consecutive years; had formed plenty of friendships but no intimate relationships; had not been able to sustain a relationship of any durability with a man; had suffered through a series of chaotic, emotionally draining holidays; and had consistently been the victim of depression and high blood pressure. As Joanne gradually let go of her emotional entanglements with her family members, she found some constructive surprises coming into her life. Her financial future brightened as she withdrew from being financially responsible for her family, and her attempts at taking risks in her relationships began to pay off. Although she still didn't have a steady man in her life and her biological clock was still ticking away, she began dating, her relationships became emotionally richer and her ability to sustain more enduring friendships grew.

As for the family, Joanne's parents and brother did not die of starvation, nor were they evicted from their home. Johnny finally realized that—guess what?—if you want to eat, you have to work! And Joanne's new detachment enabled her to see that her years of bailing the family out had kept them dependent and irresponsible.

Things That Trigger Compulsive Cycles

Joanne's acquired skill of identifying the triggers that started her compulsive cycle were instrumental in her movement toward recovery. Although the beginnings of her particular cycle were locatable in external stimuli—her mother's phone calls—there are as many triggers to behavior as there are compulsions.

As we have said, external triggers include people, places and things. Joanne's compulsion was triggered by a significant person in her life. Vanessa, whose compulsion to use credit cards we discussed in Chapter One, found that her behavior was initiated by things—mainly beautiful clothes. A glance at a lovely outfit would be the trigger that set her off on a spending spree.

Particular places can also cause knee-jerk reflexes in many cases. In his *Quantum Healing: Exploring the Frontiers of Mind/Body Medicine,* Dr. Deepak Chopra tells the story of a drug addict who was successfully recovering from his addiction when a chance occurrence threw him back into the throes of addiction. It seems that a ride on a subway train he had frequently taken in his addicted days suddenly catapulted him back into his heroin habit. The only apparent trigger was the old rickety train from bygone days. The external trigger of place can be a powerful initiator of a destructive behavior pattern.

Abundant examples of internal triggers—that is, thoughts and feelings— also exist in my practice. One woman, whose life was centered around what I call *"people-eating"* (that is, using other people to fill an inner emptiness in oneself), found that her compulsion was triggered by the thought that she would find the perfect friend, the sought-after soul mate, the person who would perfectly understand her, around the next corner. She discovered that she began every conference she went to, every professional meeting she attended with the thought that this time she would discover her other half.

AN ILLUSTRATION: MIKE'S STORY

A particularly poignant example of a compulsion triggered by a feeling is that of Mike, who engaged in the embarrassing, demeaning practice of following people from place to place. The overwhelming sense of emotional abandonment he frequently felt drove him to follow any of a number of friends and acquaintances he perceived as emotionally warm and supportive. When a particularly overwhelming sense of isolation would suddenly envelop him, he would leave his apartment, station himself outside a friend's place and wait, sometimes for hours, until his acquaintance appeared and he could follow him or her, just to feel a sense of connection.

Tracking Your Own Compulsive Pattern

Although we have detailed only one compulsion at length in this chapter, the same method that helped Joanne can be used by anyone to locate and work with the trigger that initiates his or her own compulsive behavior cycle and to become aware of and change the cycle and the pattern. The following questions are designed to help you apply the points from this chapter to your own life situation.

1. Using Joanne's case history as an example, try to identify the trigger that initiates your own compulsive activity by observing the following:

a. When do I feel a rush in my body, a sense of uncomfortable excitement, a feeling of intrusion upon my usual flow of thoughts and feelings?

b. What has occurred that has precipitated this rush, sense of excitement or anxiety, or feeling of intrusion?

c. Does this occurrence stem from an interaction with a person, from my presence in a particular place or from experience with a thing?

d. Does this occurrence seem to be related to a thought or a feeling?

2. Write out, in approximately two sentences and as clearly as you can, a description of the trigger that seems to induce a rush, a feeling of stress or the need to take an immediate and unplanned action.

3. Next, notice what set of actions proceeds from the trigger that you have just identified. Write down, in order, the observable actions that you take in response to the trigger. How many actions do you engage in? How would you characterize them? How long do they last?

4. Now that you have some sense of the behavioral cycle caused by an external or internal trigger, take note, over a specific period of time, such as a week, how many times this cycle is activated. Write down how many times it occurs.

5. Over a period of a month, notice whether there is a pattern to the cycle you have named. Some questions you might ask yourself include these:

a. Does this cycle occur in connection to work? To family events? To holidays? To visits from friends or relatives? When I have to do something I feel insecure about? When I begin something new? When I initiate a new relationship? When I go to a new place? When I go to a family reunion?

b. Can I detect a pattern having to do with my finances? Health? Work? Family? Friends? Other commitments?

Once you have identified what triggers your compulsive behavior pattern, in subsequent chapters you can learn to change your response to those triggers.

CHAPTER FOUR

Encountering
Your Feelings

When Darcy came in for her first appointment, she was angry. Angry and perplexed. A vivacious, intelligent woman in her early thirties, Darcy was a regional sales manager for a major computer company, a position she had earned through a winning combination of hard work and innate charm. It was hard to dislike Darcy. Her spontaneity and verve were infectious; her expansive enthusiasm immediately attracted both men and women, who felt warmed by her laughter, inspired by her business acumen and complimented by her attention.

Darcy had no trouble attracting friends; it was keeping them that was the problem. She went through friends the way gamblers go through money. What drove her into my office was a particularly painful betrayal by a friend of several years who suddenly, for no apparent reason, stopped returning Darcy's phone calls and suddenly vacated her apartment. Although Darcy had reported several lost or misplaced friends over the previous several months, it was this loss that stung deeply, eliciting feelings of anger and betrayal.

She did what we all do as long as we can get away with it—she blamed other people and circumstances. "Why can't I meet people who know how to be friends?" Darcy would complain. "People today just don't know how to keep commitments," she would mourn. Or "People in Massachusetts just don't know how to open up; when I go to Atlanta people there are warm and friendly."

All accusations, however, would quickly fall away as soon as a new potential friend would turn up. One day Darcy waltzed in, all smiles, from a regional sales conference she had just attended. She had finally met the perfect friend, she said. They had both grown up in Omaha, they were both 32, they both liked sky diving and they were both regional sales managers! But more important than those similarities was the instantaneous and profound feeling of "connection" that each woman had sensed from the first moment they met. Each one, Darcy said, felt that she had found her other half, her soul mate, the one other person in the world who was just the same as she.

Ensconced as she was on the pinnacle of her emotional high, Darcy was not a good candidate for dealing with a compulsion she was not yet aware she had. It would take another plummet from the giddy heights of her fantasy world to awaken Darcy to the reality of her self-defeating behavior. The plummet came soon enough, offering an opportunity for awareness and growth.

One day a troubled Darcy reported that she had spent the weekend visiting her new friend, Lisa, at her condominium complex in suburban Philadelphia. She was worried, she said, because Lisa didn't seem to get enough exercise. "What makes you think she's not getting enough exercise?" I probed. "Well, I suggested we go jogging on Saturday morning, but Lisa said she'd rather sleep in and have a leisurely brunch later. Then I said an afternoon swim would feel good, but Lisa said she preferred to see a movie at the mall. I'm worried that all this inactivity isn't good for her."

"Did you express your concern to Lisa and ask her whether she ever exercised?"

"Yes, I did. She said she doesn't exercise and she doesn't want to exercise."

"How did you feel when she said that?"

"I was shocked. How can she not want to exercise?"

As we looked together at Darcy's feelings of shock, as we probed the thoughts beneath that feeling, we found a level of extreme concern. Darcy said she wanted what was best for Lisa. So we explored what the best might be. Maybe Lisa already gets exercise, I suggested. Maybe she walks six blocks every day to the store. Maybe she climbs the stairs in her condo building or at work. Maybe she walks to the train every morning. Does Lisa look sick? No, she doesn't look sick. Has she had a physical lately? Yes, she has; she got a clean bill of health.

Our exploration of the layers beneath Darcy's concern gradually pointed the way to a reality she hadn't thought of—that perhaps her concern was unwarranted. A little reality test in the form of looking at the facts didn't substantiate the need for worry. Could it be that perhaps there was an issue here other than concern for Lisa's health? What other feelings was Darcy having about Lisa's refusal to exercise?

Well, Darcy said, it felt as if there would be less for her to share with Lisa, since exercise was so important to Darcy. There would be an area of difference. With the mention of "difference," Darcy winced. Difference was negative to her. If Lisa were somehow different from Darcy, then how could they be two halves of one whole? How could they be soul mates? How could they be just alike?

As we went deeper into the labyrinth of feelings well below the surface, we discovered that underneath Darcy's belief that she was concerned only for her friend's health was an unconscious concern of much greater magnitude—concern for herself and her fantasy of finding a soul mate, someone she had characterized as "just like me." Concern for Lisa's health was merely the face her fantasy wore. Any difference between Darcy and Lisa became an instantaneous threat, dangerous to admit into reality because it meant death to the fantasy "we're just alike."

Darcy's exploration led her to the tough realization that she was a compulsive people-eater. The reason she kept losing friends was not that people in Massachusetts didn't know how to share. It was that she was emotionally voracious. In the beginning people would be attracted to this charming, successful, well-dressed woman, but in almost every instance her relationships would not last beyond six months. Why? People-eaters aren't looking for real relationship or sharing. They are looking for extensions of themselves—someone they can objectify into whatever they need to take away the burden of loneliness. After a few hard months of deep work, that's what Darcy and I realized was the root of her problem—the fear of being alone.

As Darcy continued her hard work in therapy, she began to realize that her compulsive people-eating pattern had been her unconscious way of keeping her fearful feelings at bay. As long as she entertained the fantasy that a magical soul mate could save her from her inevitable aloneness, she could postpone experiencing her own fears—fears of abandonment, of being alone, of getting old, of being the only person responsible for her life.

Typically, Darcy's pattern would start in a situation such as a sales conference, where she would automatically and unconsciously "scan" the participants, waiting for the internal "click" that heralded the feeling of connection, of magnetism, of being on the same wavelength. Flattered by her attention, Darcy's new acquaintance would warm to the flame of her proffered friendship, and off Darcy would soar—until the cycle inevitably ended in a crashing feeling of betrayal and desertion. Darcy's perplexity was real; she didn't understand that her acquaintances felt annoyed, trapped, caught. As soon as they attempted to assert their own identity, they ruined her fantasy and the relationship was demolished.

As Darcy began to be aware that she was continually scanning her environment, waiting for the rush produced by finding someone she thought was "just the same," she was able to detect the trigger that set off the cycle and then to track the pattern her behavior took. She was able to see that a particular type of vital, attractive young woman personified the notion "She's just like me" and set off the emotional high. The feeling during this high was "I'll never be alone again; my isolation will be over forever." The people-eating was never about relationship; it was only about veiling the fear of being alone. Although the inevitable crash that followed the appearance of differences was excruciating, Darcy was able to see how she had caused it by her compulsive behavior. Encountering her fear, accepting it, taking responsibility for it and finding creative ways to express it and deal with it enabled Darcy to break her long chain of aborted "relationships."

Darcy learned to stop spending energy on controlling others—on trying to get them to stay just like her. Because she was willing to go through the pain of encountering her deepest feelings, she was eventually able to give up her lifelong fantasy: "If I could unzip this person from head to toe, I would walk right in, I would fit perfectly and we would be just the same. I'd find another me." By laying claim to her own fear, Darcy has paved the way for real friendships where only counterfeits existed before.

◇◇◇

As we shall see throughout this chapter, underneath all our compulsive behavior patterns lie deeply buried emotions waiting for us to discover them and set them free. If we befriend them in the right way, they will serve us bountifully; if we neglect and despise them, they will cripple us.

Compulsions as Expressions of Our Hidden Feelings

All human beings have feelings, and when those feelings are not expressed in an open, healthy way, they will be expressed in an unhealthy, hidden way. I once read an article about a small boy abandoned in a ghetto apartment by his drug-addicted parents. During the several days before rescuers found him, the child, who had quickly devoured all the food in the kitchen, turned to eating plaster, paper and even pillows to assuage his hunger. Like this little boy who stuffed whatever was available into his mouth so that he wouldn't feel his hunger, we, too, use anything that is available to us, no matter how self-destructive or devious, to express our feelings. Often the only thing available is a compulsive behavior pattern. It is only when we encounter the buried feeling that is taking such a distorted avenue of expression that we begin to get to the root of our compulsive cycle so we can start to change it.

All human beings get hungry; all need food. What they eat depends on a variety of factors—where they live, what the culture says is appropriate to eat, what the economic considerations are and numerous other factors. Likewise, the expression of feelings is dependent on a number of variables. Human beings will express—or not express—their feelings depending on the environment and circumstances that surround them.

LAYERING OF FEELINGS

In my practice I have found that, generally speaking, the feelings we experience as uncomfortable are layered inside us in a way that is fairly predictable. The first layer that usually surfaces is anger; the next is sadness, and the last is fear. Although anger usually springs from feeling hurt and afraid, it is often used as a defense to protect us from feeling the deeper level of unbearable vulnerability. So the anger is like armor; it can be used as a survival mechanism, as a protection or even as a form of attack. It can scare people away from us, exempting us from expressing our own fear—but only temporarily.

Although sadness is a more precarious feeling than anger, it still makes us feel less vulnerable than fear does. We can feel sad and at the same time feel some kind of strength and power. But fear, the deepest layer of all, is the most difficult for people to deal with because we are often unable to mobilize any personal power as a defense when we are feeling it. Not only does it place us in a condition of emotional vulnerability; it also causes us to feel physiologically vulnerable. We find our hands shaking, our jaws quivering and our insides turned to jelly. Usually fear comes from one of two sources: from the sense of being abandoned by others or from the sense of being abandoned by oneself. As such, fear can involve a sense of either emotional or physical annihilation, isolation and pain.

Although, as I have said, the usual emotional peeling-away process moves from anger through sadness to fear, not every client encounters his or her feelings in this order. Some people have been brought up with such stigmas attached to anger that it is unthinkable for them to express rage or hostility until they have been in therapy for a while. Such clients often enter therapy with sadness as the most accessible emotion. They will cry first and mobilize their anger later. Although quite a rare occurrence, still other clients will enter therapy with fear right beneath the surface. Usually these people are in the process of what we call "bottoming out." They may have tried and tried and tried again to deal with their compulsions; they may have totally lost control or any sense of direction; their compulsions may have achieved complete power over them, and their lives, as the twelve-step programs say, may have become "unmanageable." When clients come into therapy in the grips of such desperate circumstances, I will often do some strengthening work with them so their egos are sound enough to withstand the hard, painful work of getting to the root of their compulsive behaviors.

FEELINGS AND THEIR VARIATIONS

Feelings are like colors—there are primary ones and secondary ones, and then there are infinite blendings that produce the subtlest of variations. Anger, sadness and fear are the primary emotions, but they overlap and blend in countless individual and unique ways. In my experience shame, embarrassment, jealousy, rage, grief and a host of other feelings are all variations of the three primary emotions I see in clients. Dana, the perpetual seductress, arrived in my office in literal pain, the discomfort in her neck apparently caused by tension. Then she moved into anger—at her boyfriends, her family and me. Finally, as she confronted her compulsion and the possibility of living without her customary identity, she encountered fear.

Harry, the movie binger, came into my office in depression (which is sadness and anger turned inward), then moved to overt anger (first at me), a sense of betrayal (a form of pain or sadness) by his family and finally fear. Joanne, the rescuer, entered therapy feeling a blending of pain and anger at missing vacations and then moved into fear at the idea of "losing" her family, a family that she had lost long ago without ever realizing it. And Darcy, the people-eater, came to see me because of anger over a lost relationship and a sense of betrayal (sadness and fear) by friends. She confronted her fear last as she contemplated life alone without the fantasy of someone "just like me."

Compulsions as Attempts to Achieve Balance

Healthy people lead balanced lives. Human beings innately long for balance, and when we can't achieve it in creative, fulfilling ways, we try to attain it in ways that frequently have destructive consequences. Compensation is one way of trying to achieve balance. Most of us have experienced the principle of compensation on a very basic level. Some of us have a tendency to "reward" ourselves when we're feeling blue by eating or drinking too much or by splurging on expenditures our pocketbooks really can't afford. Many parents, after overreacting to their children's whining or temper tantrums, have made unplanned purchases at the toy store or taken excursions to the ice cream shop. Sometimes our compensations are appropriate and help restore the balance we're seeking, but sometimes they unwittingly tip the scales further in the direction in which we were already headed.

Because destructive mood-altering behaviors are attempts at compensations—that is, unconscious efforts to restore balance—it is important to find out what they are compensating for if we are to discard them and bring real harmony and balance to life. As I said in Chapter One, mood-altering behaviors are ways of dealing with or expressing feelings that are blocked for whatever reason. Perhaps in the childhood situations in which the feelings were first experienced the anger, sadness and fear were so powerful that they couldn't be expressed without dire consequences. The only safe way to deal with them might have been through diversionary tactics, such as mood-altering behaviors.

What compensatory mood-altering behaviors people use to avoid feeling their feelings depends on a variety of factors. The nature of the circumstances they grew up in, their reactions to these circumstances, the nature of the feelings that could not be expressed and the availability of "safe" options for expressing their feelings in alternative ways—all play a part in the unconscious, slow development of mood-altering behaviors.

AN ILLUSTRATION: MIKE'S STORY

Mike, the compulsive follower who was described briefly in the last chapter, grew up in a fairly affluent suburban home. Although all his material needs were provided for, Mike was emotionally bereft. As the only child of two professionals who were home infrequently, he led an often excruciatingly lonely existence. Even when his parents did spend an occasional evening or weekend at home, Mike's weak complaints of feeling friendless were met with disbelief. His parents were sure he was just being a spoiled brat. Didn't he have everything money could buy? Mike's intense feelings of emotional abandonment and loneliness were unacceptable, and soon he himself wondered if his parents were correct in thinking he was ungrateful. His feelings became more and more hidden, less and less admissible—to himself as well as to everyone else in his life.

When Mike came to see me, it took him quite a long time to admit a behavior he was perplexed and embarrassed by. He had an uncontrollable urge to follow his friends. The pattern we were able to piece together revealed that at the slightest instance of disagreement in a friendly relationship, Mike would hit the panic button. If he couldn't spend time with his friend or get in contact by phone, he would walk to his friend's home or apartment complex and wait—sometimes for hours, even in the pouring rain—for his friend to leave the building. Then he would follow him around town, dodging behind buildings, ducking into alleyways, diving into phone booths. There was something about being in proximity to his friend that made him feel less anxious, less abandoned, more in control. Because his friend was in sight, Mike felt calmer; he had a sense of not being alone. He felt that he and his friend were together, even though they were not; he felt safe, even though he was hiding out in a phone booth. If his friend disappeared around a corner, his anxiety would build again, culminating in the feeling of total aloneness. Although he had a deep feeling of abandonment, Mike could not have verbalized it. All he felt was nameless anxiety and fear that was relieved by keeping his friend in sight. This particular compulsion, because it was so demeaning, was difficult even to admit to, let alone work with.

A CLOSER LOOK AT MIKE'S BEHAVIOR

How do we see the variables involved in a mood-altering behavior played out in Mike's story? First, in the nature of his circumstances: Mike's home life was dead on a feeling level; he received no emotional nourishment or warmth from his family. Second, in Mike's reaction to his circumstances: Mike felt emotionally starved and tried to express his needs to his parents, but his parents rejected and even denied his feelings, failing to acknowledge their validity. Third, in his emotional life: Mike felt abandoned, alone, cut off—and for good reason. Finally, the variables involved in Mike's mood-altering behavior were played out in the availability of options for expressing his feelings: Mike could not find any healthy ways of expressing his feelings of abandonment since he was told that (a) his circumstances were ideal and he should be grateful and (b) his feelings were "inaccurate" and therefore inappropriate. No one had ever "mirrored" for Mike. That is, no one had ever reflected his feelings back to him, acknowledging their validity. Instead he had been taught to label his feelings of abandonment and pain as ingratitude. He thought he must be to blame for the loneliness and abandonment he felt. As the pressure of loneliness escalated in his adolescent years, Mike developed a compulsive behavior pattern as the only way to forestall the feelings of abandonment that always threatened to overwhelm him. Following his friends made him feel safe and powerful.

Mood-Altering Behaviors and Control

In addition to being misguided attempts to create balance, mood-altering behaviors are also ways of controlling feelings. Twelve-step programs often talk about "surrender" or an admission of "powerlessness" as a vital part of recovery. Such an admission is also important in dealing with mood-altering behaviors. As long as we try to "control" our real feelings by counteracting them with destructive behaviors, we have little chance of getting to the root cause of our problems and making choices that change our patterns. People-eating was Darcy's way of controlling her silent need for intimacy; seduction was Dana's way of controlling the feeling of powerlessness that originated in her relationship with her father; Mike's compulsion to follow people kept his fear of abandonment under lock and key—all with destructive consequences, however. The distraction provided by the compulsion—the sensation of being powerful through seduction, of approximating intimacy through people-eating, of being in proximity through following—gave each person the illusion that he or she was in control—when, in fact, each one was out of control.

The sensations experienced through a compulsive behavior pattern cannot be mistaken for the real feelings they are concealing. As we have noted, a compulsion is the way we try to create an external balance, through our behavior, that is not present internally, on a feeling level. The intensity and pervasiveness of the compulsion indicate the depth of the feelings inside. Some of my clients, instead of engaging in mood-altering behaviors, have conscious mood-altering fantasies that serve as substitutes, as ways of attempting to achieve balance and maintain control. Although they may not be as destructive as overt behaviors, mood-altering fantasies nevertheless keep people from confronting their feelings and taking authentic control of their lives. Everyone has fantasies, but when our fantasizing becomes compulsive, we are heading for trouble.

The "Flip Factor"

As I have already explained, my experiences with my clients have taught me that there is a common layering of uncomfortable emotions that frequently manifest themselves in a particular order in therapy—namely anger, sadness and fear. Although there are variations to that layering, most clients eventually deal with all three emotions, or blendings of those emotions—and also pleasant feelings such as joy and love—by the time they conclude their psychological work.

What is less clear and less predictable, however, is the relationship between the feeling that has been repressed for years as a result of painful experiences and the particular compulsion that develops in response to that repressed feeling. However, I have noticed what I call the *"flip factor"*: we may externally create a behavior that reflects the opposite of whatever's going on inside. We may flip an internal feeling of powerlessness into a compulsion that reflects a powerful stance. We may flip intense fear into its opposite, excitement. Anger, which is sometimes expressed as a component of depression, may be reflected in a compulsion characterized by passivity, such as compulsive television watching or Harry's compulsive movie binging.

Our own sadness, pain or grief may be flipped over into sadness, pain or grief about friends or family members and may be expressed in a compulsion such as rescuing. Joanne, whose story was told in Chapter Three, was experiencing deep pain about her unacknowledged feelings of being taken advantage of by her family, of being without a family. As long as she was compulsively rescuing her parents and brother, getting an emotional high every time she powerfully rushed in to save the day in a crisis situation, she did not feel her own grief and sadness.

Of course there is no nice, neat, predictable correlation between a given feeling and a particular compulsion. Not all rescuers are expressing pain, and not all television watchers are angry and full of passive-aggressive behaviors. As I have already said, feelings have shades and variations, and so do their contorted expressions through compulsive channels. To some degree, all three of the major categories of uncomfortable emotions are expressed in behavior patterns, although the degree of emphasis varies. It is fascinating to notice the human story implicit in each compulsive activity—the nature of the compulsive behavior, what feelings it is expressing in a skewed manner and the nature of the correlation between the behavior and the feelings.

DAN'S STORY: THWARTING FEAR BY COURTING DANGER

One way to thwart, to disallow, feelings of fear and powerlessness is to choose dangerous situations that allow us to challenge our human limits, proving that we're not afraid, that we're powerful. Dan lived near a large lake. At two o'clock one morning he found himself compelled to get up out of bed and go row a boat out onto the lake in the midst of a terrible thunderstorm. It was pitch black except for the sudden bolts of lightning that streaked through the sky, but there Dan sat in torrents of pounding rain, feeling exhilarated and triumphant. By flying in the face of danger, even possible death, Dan was asserting his power. He was daring the elements to kill him; he was challenging nature, and his victory made him feel immortal, fearless, in control. Although his challenges to the universe were not always this daring, Dan nevertheless was frequently compelled to be involved in dangerous, even life-threatening, situations that momentarily produced a sensation of power and excitement, staving off his deeply hidden feelings of powerlessness and fear.

CHARLOTTE'S STORY: DRESSING SMART
TO KEEP FROM FEELING STUPID

Although most compulsions are appropriately compensatory, not all are equally destructive or inappropriate. Charlotte had a constant, inordinate focus on clothing that was her way of compensating for deep-seated feelings of inadequacy. Incessantly criticized as a child by her brilliant father, Charlotte had been routinely told she was stupid—a cardinal sin in her family. As an adult, Charlotte was obsessed with the idea of "looking smart." Hers was not a spending or a charging compulsion; the high did not come from the act of purchasing. Rather, it was the assembling and wearing of a "smart" outfit that gave Charlotte a sense of well-being and control over her imagined mental defectiveness. Having smart clothes in her closet, being able to dress smartly for any occasion, was Charlotte's protection against the feelings of stupidity that had constantly assailed her as a child and adolescent.

JERRY'S STORY: BEATING THE CLOCK
TO AVOID BEING ORDINARY

A big part of Jerry's life was centered around "beating the clock." If he had an appointment scheduled for 10:00 a.m., he would plan his morning to make sure he got to his destination about two minutes before 10:00. It was not fun, he claimed, to get there at ten minutes to 10:00. "Anybody can get there ten minutes early," said Jerry. Only a special person could time everything right—getting in the car, backing down the driveway, going through morning traffic, finding a parking space and walking to the office building— with only 120 seconds to spare. It was always very exciting to cut ahead of a car on the expressway, to beat a light at a major intersection. A fairly consistent state of suspense kept Jerry feeling high as he wondered if he could maneuver through the myriad obstacles on his route and still get there 120 seconds ahead of time. If he got to his appointment more than 120 seconds early, or if he got there late, he felt a depressing sense of letdown, a feeling of boredom. "It feels like nothing," he would say when I questioned him about the letdown. "It feels boring and empty."

Although Jerry's way of avoiding the feelings of ordinariness, emptiness and boredom was to "beat the clock," ensuring that his life was special, full and exciting, there are numerous similar avenues to the same end. Nan, a freelance book designer who lived in the suburbs, lined up all her appointments in the city so she wouldn't have any extra space on her calendar, no empty time slots. The prospect of empty space, of unplanned time, was too frightening to Nan, whose feelings of emptiness and abandonment were kept at bay by an overly full schedule.

Learning to Identify Feelings

Because compulsions are directly related to unexpressed, usually unconscious, feelings that have been "safely" kept at bay for years, one of the first steps in the recovery process is learning to identify those feelings. After we have learned to recognize that a compulsive behavior is affecting our lives (Chapter Two) and then detected the pattern or cycle the behavior takes (Chapter Three), then it's time to turn detective and start our personal and familial clue-gathering. Where did this compulsion come from? What feelings are we trying to avoid? What events in our personal history gave rise to these feelings?

LEARNING FROM YOUR COMPULSIONS

Our compulsions have something very important to teach us. The attitude we adopt toward them is crucial, for if we approach them with respect, with the belief that they have something to reveal to us, then we will learn whatever we need to. We won't learn anything if we get compulsive about recovering from our compulsions! So the first step is to take the compulsive behavior seriously, to watch it, go into it, probe it, examine it. To start with, try to answer the following questions:

1. How would you describe your compulsion in one sentence?

2. What is this behavior trying to show you?

3. What clues in the description can lead you toward the feeling underneath the compulsion?

  a. Do you compulsively fill up your time like Nan? If so, is the feeling one of emptiness?

  b. Do you constantly court excitement by speeding, tailgating or weaving in and out of traffic? If so, is the feeling one of fear?

  c. Do you insist on being right in every discussion you're involved in? If so, do you feel somewhere deep inside that you are always wrong, defective or inferior to others?

4. What might your compulsion be compensating for?

Since you are now aware that a compulsive behavior is affecting your life and since you have become aware of its pattern, watch for clues to your feelings at the onset of your compulsive behavior, during its cycle and in its aftermath. What feeling is hiding underneath the emotional high, the sensation the compulsion provides? If you are a shopper like Vanessa, does the feeling that you can buy whatever you need give you a sensation of power followed by a feeling of powerlessness? Are you compelled to engage in behavior that makes you "look smart" when you really feel stupid or ashamed, like Charlotte, who compensated with her elegant wardrobe? By adopting the stance of a skillful detective, a cunning sleuth, you can become a great observer, informed by the details and clues you keep picking up.

TUNING IN TO YOUR BODY

One of the most important arenas we can learn to become aware of is that of the body. By tuning in to our bodies—by focusing on what sensations, pains, tensions and other feelings we can notice in our bodies—we raise our awareness of our emotions. Although we are starting to understand that our bodies and minds operate together, that they constitute aspects of one whole system, we still tend to be dualistic in our responses. I once asked participants in a workshop I led to jump up into the air while raising their arms and yelling "I'm depressed!" Everyone collapsed into laughter; the absurd disparity between the bodily expression and the words was obvious. On the other hand, if we try to repeat the words "I'm depressed" with some sense of conviction, we will discover that our voices will slow down, our breathing will become more shallow, our bodies may feel heavier, our heads may bow down, our eyes will drop and our intonation will be lower. A complete behavior change ensues when the interior feeling changes.

Conversely, if you tell someone, "I'm excited!" your eyes will probably open wider, your voice will speed up, your posture will be a little more erect and your movement will be quicker. It is impossible to separate bodily movement and gesture from inner disposition. Observing our bodies is thus an excellent way to find clues to feelings we may not be aware of. I often pick up many initial clues about my clients merely from their body language.

Actual physical pain can also provide clues to our feelings. Dana, the seductress, was referred to me by a specialist who could find no organic reason for her neck pain. This pain was on the left side of her neck. It has been found that people who are unable to express their emotions often experience pain on the side of their body with which they would normally lash out. Dana was left-handed. If she had been able to lash out it would have been with her left hand. It is significant that when she learned to express her emotions, her pain disappeared.

A mental health counselor whose professional helping mindset invaded his entire life until he was "fixing" every situation in his personal relationships, too, used to unconsciously twist the pillows of my office couch into tight, angry knots and then complain that the joints in his hands hurt. It is no secret that high blood pressure is connected to stress and tension, as are many other afflictions whose relationships to feelings are not so universally proven. As the ailments of our bodies may express our feelings, instead of feeling our emotions themselves we often *somatize* them, which means that we express our emotional distress through our bodies.

As we cultivate awareness, we will discover other clues located in our body-mind system. We will start to notice little signs that something uncomfortable is happening. We may feel a tightening in the neck or shoulders, a constriction or dryness in the throat, an edge of nausea in the gut, a flutter in the heart. We may notice the same kinds of emotional flurries Joanne felt when she was watching her rescuing pattern move into action with her mother on the phone. Different people will notice different signs according to their personal backgrounds, their family histories and their current circumstances.

LEARNING TO TRUST YOUR FEELINGS

Identifying these bodily feelings will move us closer and closer to being able to actually identify the emotions that we are trying to block when we go into compulsion formation. Our bodies don't lie; it's just that we're not used to trusting them. One of the forms of denial we can easily take is to second-guess our bodily feelings and our gut reactions. The body may be saying, "This hurts; this hurts!" And the mind may respond, "This is not happening; this is not happening!" The more we intellectualize and rationalize our pain, the less we trust our bodies and instinctual wisdom and the more split and compulsive we become. If we pay attention to the facts of our experience and our body wisdom, we will discover our awareness of feelings increasing.

I'll never forget an experience reported by a friend who was recalling her high school days. She described an English course on how to write a research paper. When the teacher asked the class what they would do if they found their research did not support a particular hypothesis, one young man raised his hand and said, in all seriousness, "Change the facts, of course!"

We are frequently so blinded by an unexamined life hypothesis we have that we cannot see the facts, the clues, that are staring us in the face. The body, the gut, will say, "Something's going on here that's suspicious." And the mind will interpret this observation, saying, "I must be crazy, because nothing could be going on here." If we risk changing our hypothesis, if we admit that the facts may be right—something suspicious *is* going on here— we may find ourselves on the road to encountering our feelings, to trusting our own observations and our instincts. In return, however, we will probably have to sacrifice the beloved hypothesis we have given lip service to all our lives.

It is that hypothesis that is the backbone of our unconscious fantasy (see Chapter Five), and we have protected it with our lives at the cost of our lives. When Joanne began to become aware of the facts about her mother's phone calls, when she began to hear what her mother was really saying, she had to sacrifice the fantasy that her family would be able to express their caring for her. The facts broke her family trance, but they also freed her from her compulsion to indiscriminately rescue. Freedom came, however, only after Joanne encountered her feelings—feelings of abandonment, loneliness and betrayal.

ENCOUNTERING YOUR FEELINGS

The cost of encountering our feelings can be very high, but ultimately the price is well worth it. One woman whose entire relationship history was with unreliable, manipulative men finally broke her pattern by taking the clues she saw at face value. Susan's boyfriend swore that he loved her, showered her with gifts and charmed her out of her increasingly frequent despondencies. Frequently shunted aside at the last minute so that her man could spend time with his mother, Susan said she felt guilty about her gut reactions of hurt and anger. "His mother is very nice to me," she would insist. "Frank is such a good son, and I know I shouldn't feel upset, but it's just that I spend every Saturday evening alone."

One day I suggested that Susan and I do some role-playing. "I'll be you and you be Frank," I directed. It was only when Susan could hear herself—as Frank—say, "I love you so much, Susan, I really love you, but I have to go now, because I'm meeting my mother again tonight for dinner," that she was finally able to experience the contradiction between Frank's words and his behavior. Her realization broke her fantasy, the spell that had captivated her. Her much-needed hypothesis was that Frank loved her; therefore, the facts were wrong. She couldn't be hurting inside because Frank loved her and because his mother was so nice to her. He wouldn't mistreat her, so her instincts must be wrong. When Susan was finally willing to tear the veil off of this reality, she was able to encounter her feelings of pain and anger directly and confront Frank. Tuning into the facts—and her own feelings—cost Susan her illusion but gave her back her own reality. It was the beginning of more healthy relationships for this young woman.

REALITY TESTING

We can do some reality testing about our feelings by listening to what we verbalize. There are a number of helpful contexts for doing so. One is in the presence of a therapist who can reflect what we say, act as a mirror for us and lead us into a perception of patterns we may see more clearly with some expert guidance. Another place we can hear ourselves verbalize our feelings is in a support group. There are numerous groups available today—twelve-step programs and others—that offer safe places for people to hear themselves and others identify what is going on with them internally.

We can learn to listen to ourselves, watching our own language for clues that will reveal what is going on under the surface. Repeated statements expressing doubt, such as "I don't know if I can . . . " or projections of negative outcomes to current dilemmas often reveal fear. Constant repetitions of "I wish" statements often indicate an underlying sadness or feelings of loss. Habitual recalling of days when things were better, people were more considerate and life was more rewarding may suggest feelings of victimization or abandonment. Expressions of envy, of having less than others, often indicate hidden feelings of anger and fear. People who continually say they "feel sorry for" others may be projecting their own sadness elsewhere so they don't have to feel it for themselves.

Incessant statements of comparison often point to feelings of powerlessness or a sense of being "less than." Black-and-white assertions such as "You always" or "You never" and frequent use of "should" and "ought" statements and other judgments often indicate anger and a sense of inferiority that are concealed underneath an exterior of moral superiority.

DEALING WITH WHAT YOU FIND

Once we have pulled back the veil from our muffled feelings, we will have to deal with what we find. Given that we may not have really felt our feelings for years—given that our emotions have been shut down, sealed off, locked up because it was not safe to feel them—we will need strategies for educating, channeling and expressing our feelings, for they are likely to have some of the characteristics of five-year-olds or fourteen-year-olds or people of whatever age we were when we shut down. Such strategies will be offered in the *Recovery* section of this book in Chapters Eight, Nine and Ten. Meanwhile, the feelings we uncover are clues to the unconscious fantasies we created in response to our childhood environments. We must find out about these fantasies if we are serious about leaving our compulsions behind us.

PART THREE

Clarification

CHAPTER FIVE

Discovering
Your Unconscious Fantasy

Like the proverbial man in Chapter Two who customarily fell into the pothole on his way to work, we, too, have customarily fallen into our compulsive behavior patterns, usually unaware of what we were doing and certainly not realizing there was a way around the pothole, or even another road to travel.

In Part Two, *Awareness*, we learned to identify the compulsions that hold power over our lives, we learned to examine and track their cycles, and then we learned to identify the hidden, unrecognized feelings for which these compulsions in some way compensate.

Having become aware of the fact that compulsions exist, that they have a pattern and that they operate in response to circumstances that encouraged us to block certain emotions, we can move on in this section to the clarification process.

Compulsions are clues to the presence of unnamed, unknown, unmet feelings that originate, almost always, in childhood. When we first encounter these muffled feelings, they are likely to have a potency that is out of proportion to our current life experience. What we can discover through clarification is the reason for that potency, for the disproportionate nature of that feeling.

Awareness shows us the condition we are in today; clarification shows us how we got that way; recovery, as we shall discover in Part Four, shows us how we can use our understanding of the past and our experience in the present to change the future. Or, to use the analogy of the pothole, in the process of awareness we realize that there are potholes we keep falling into, in the process of clarification we discover that we can walk down the road without always falling into these potholes and in recovery we learn increasingly to stay out of the potholes, although we may occasionally still fall in.

In Part Three we will find out that feelings come from somewhere in particular, that we do not arbitrarily invent or concoct them and that we are not being perverse when we admit them into consciousness when we feel angry, sad, ashamed or fearful. We will come to understand that our feelings— or their apparent absence—were reactions to circumstances that we ourselves did not create and that were not our fault. More important, we will also begin to see that we don't have to spend the rest of our lives in reaction, that we can change patterns from the past—but only if we first see them and understand how they came to be. We can choose to change our patterns. We can cease to live life as a reaction. We can take appropriate responsibility for the future.

The Roles
of Our Unconscious Fantasies

Our unconscious fantasies fulfill many roles in our lives. Some of the most common are described below.

FULFILLING OUR WISHES

According to the *American Heritage Dictionary of the English Language*, the meaning of the word fantasy is "an imagined event or condition fulfilling a wish." Darcy's people-eating compulsion revealed her unconscious fantasy, her imagined condition fulfilling a wish. Her need for emotional connection and self-verification was so great that she wished to have a relationship that concretely personified the meeting of this need. So she attempted to create, through her voracious appetite for new friends, the conditions that would fulfill this need, this wish for connection. She believed that, if she could just find the perfect friend, she would be validated and loneliness would be banished forever. With the appearance of her long-awaited soul mate, she would be snatched from her emotional void. Darcy's continuous, compulsive search for this imaginary person was doomed to failure, for conditions invented to fulfill a wish are out of step with reality.

PROTECTING US FROM HARD-TO-FACE REALITIES

Joanne, who compulsively rescued her family from crisis after crisis, had held fast to her unconscious fantasy all her life, for its death would have forced her to see a reality that was hard to face: that her family had used her for their own ends while verbally maintaining that they didn't want to involve her in their problems.

Joanne's fantasy that she could create the family she needed—that she had parents and a brother who, though beleaguered by misfortune, had her best interests at heart—was repeatedly expressed in her rescuing stance. Only when the collision between the facts and her fantasy became excruciatingly obvious to Joanne could she start to see that she had created an imaginary scenario that was an attempt to fulfill her wish for a supportive family.

MAINTAINING ORDER IN THE MIDST OF CHAOS

To maintain some kind of order in the midst of the secrecy and chaos of her formative years, Dana, who seduced men who later left her, had created one of the most magical fantasies a woman can have: that of a princess whose charm and seductive powers are legendary.

Although Dana was, indeed, charming and seductive, she believed that this charm could bring her anything she wanted. She had not yet realized that what she really wanted, acceptance of the self beneath the glamorous package, could not be obtained through seduction.

ENLARGING OUR SENSE OF SELF

Dan, who courted danger by taking a boat out onto a lake in the middle of raging thunderstorms, maintained his unconscious fantasy of omnipotence by walking the tightrope between life and death in dangerous situations. Each time that he emerged unscathed from a precarious encounter, his fantasy of personal power and immortality grew larger, fed by the experiences he kept accumulating.

Dan's compulsion to create crises revealed, over and over, his wish to be larger than life, to be "more than," compensating for the sense of being "less than" that he had felt growing up.

CREATING A SENSE OF SAFETY

Mike, who compulsively followed people from place to place throughout the city, had had a childhood with no sense of emotional safety. The only way he could stave off the tremendous sense of insecurity and danger he experienced was to keep in sight someone with whom he felt an emotional connection. His fantasy was "I can keep people from abandoning me."

HELPING US SURVIVE INTENSE PAIN

Susan's fantasy about her relationship with her lover, Frank, was that she was the most important woman in his life. It was only after she tested her hypothesis against the unrelenting facts of Frank's behavior that she came to the unwelcome conclusion that she was not number one. The pain of feeling unreciprocated love, which had been Susan's experience while growing up, spawned the fantasy that she was valued by the successive men in her life. Only when Susan was strong enough to accept the truth of her place in their lives was she able to identify her unconscious fantasy, give it up and move on.

The Characteristics
of Our Unconscious Fantasies

Although it is the nature of our personal experiences and the idiosyncrasies of our formative circumstances that govern the creation of our unconscious fantasies, there are certain basic characteristics that virtually all fantasies, as we have defined them, have in common:

1. The fantasy is out of step with reality.
2. The fantasy perpetuates controlling behavior.
3. The fantasy is reactive instead of active, keeping us stuck.
4. The fantasy is indicative of the underlying belief system we hold.

These characteristics are most readily understood when they are seen in the stories of real people who have struggled with their compulsive behaviors and the unconscious fantasies in whose soil the compulsions took root and flourished.

OUT OF STEP WITH REALITY: NOREEN'S STORY

One of my clients, Noreen, told the following story: "During the first few years of my life, my family had quite a bit of money and I always felt like we were the aristocrats of the town where we lived. My mother redecorated once a year and we pretty much bought whatever we wanted. But when my parents were divorced and my mother took a low-paying job, things changed. I remember bill collectors knocking at our door. I felt so ashamed. But my mother still bought beautiful clothes, even when she didn't pay the rent on time.

"I started working when I was fifteen, and I remember opening up charge accounts right away. Whatever store would give me a card, I got one. I had them all. I learned to live beyond my means. I've lived that way all my life, and I still do. Sometimes I'll go a few weeks without charging anything, but then I get so anxious that I just rush out and go on a real spree. If I haven't charged anything for a while, I start feeling like I don't have enough, that I need to get something. Sometimes I think, 'If I can just get this one thing I want, I'll be fixed.'

"When I go shopping, I usually have something in mind that I want to buy, but once I get in the store everything opens up and I buy anything that suits me. Over the last few years, my salary has really increased, but what I've been doing is buying on sale so I can get twice as much. I mostly go on Saturdays, either for an hour or two or for the whole day. It'll often occur to me in the middle of the week, 'Oh good, I have no plans for Saturday. I think I'll just hit the stores and see what the sales are.' I know it's sick, but I want to hold onto it. It's a way of getting high.

"When I visit my family, we all go shopping. I go shopping with my mother, with my aunt and even with my grandmother. We all live beyond our means, we're all in debt. Most of my life I've lain awake at night wondering how I was going to pay the bills. I used to think, 'Oh, God, I wish somebody would just come and take care of me. I could just turn my paycheck over to them and they would give me an allowance.' I'm a little better off now than I used to be, because last year I made six figures. But I'm still not saving for my future, and my foundation is very shaky. I have stashed away some savings, but I know my paycheck isn't going to get me through until my next bonus and I'm going to have to take at least $1,000 a month out to supplement my income to pay my charge accounts.

"I mostly charge clothes for work and for casual wear. My wardrobe swings aren't quite as dramatic now that I don't go out and hit the bars like I used to. But I still buy expensive clothes for work and for fun. I guess I'm always looking for the perfect outfit. Other people seem to have a flair for dressing. They always look like they just stepped out of a bandbox. I always feel like a mess, no matter how expensive my clothes are. Lately I've started to realize that it's because I don't know how to dress myself. I don't know my style. But I always think, 'Maybe this next outfit will do it, will fix me.' And if I'm fixed—well, maybe I'll feel good about myself, or maybe I'll get married, or maybe the boss will love me.

"I think there are so many things I don't want to feel, so many things that might be painful, that when I get near them I just rush out and charge things. It's worked for a long time. Every once in a while I chop up the credit cards. But after a few days I call up and get new ones."

DISCOVERING NOREEN'S FANTASY

Because Noreen had done some work on herself (she was in a support group, had had some therapy and wanted to change), she had developed some awareness of her compulsion (charge-card abuse), its origins (all the women in her family made it a way of life) and her fantasy ("If I can get the right outfit, I'll be fixed"). Noreen's behavior pattern is a particularly good example of the first characteristic we have listed of the fantasies that provide a context for compulsive behaviors. Her fantasy was out of touch with reality because charging couldn't fix her, but it was also out of touch because she spent almost as much as she earned, because she was not saving for the future and because her charging promoted unhealthy, compulsion-based family relationships.

Noreen's recognition that her behavior was out of touch with reality was a move in the right direction, but it hadn't yet changed her unrealistic behavior. She was still at an early stage of awareness, seeing the pothole but constantly falling in. Her fantasy was particularly entrenched because she had so many role models for it and it was so acceptable.

At least Noreen was able to identify the feelings of anxiety, shame and pain that came up when she wasn't charging, when her compulsion wasn't taking her emotional energy and "saving" her from her feelings. And she knew that the repeated enactment of her compulsive cycle was an embodiment of the fantasy "I'll be fixed." Even though she never felt permanently "fixed" after succumbing to her compulsion, she engaged in it again and again anyway, indulging herself in the fantasy that even though she hadn't yet been fixed, one of these days she would be.

Unlike many others, Noreen was aware of her own fantasy. She was able to verbalize "I don't know this person, so of course I don't know how to dress this person." The fantasy was that she would be able to be fixed by charging, and to give up charging was to admit that it couldn't fix her. To change her behavior Noreen had to accept herself the way she was realistically, without fixing, without charging. She was finally able to do that, though she had to experience more pain before she was willing to give up this deeply rooted compulsion.

PERPETUATING CONTROLLING BEHAVIOR: DAVE'S AND NORMAN'S STORIES

When Dave first came to see me, he told this story: "I over-exercise. I have a club I go to, and I'm there all the time, often once a day at least for two hours. Sometimes I miss important meetings because of exercise, which is not good, but there is a high I get from working out that makes me feel good. It's a nice high, but it makes me feel like I don't need to go to a meeting. I tell people all the time that if they're not exercising, they should be. I probably do it too much. Sometimes I'll go more than once a day. I get compulsive about my weight, too, about keeping fit. I'll go through a day where I'll be tired and still push myself until I'm totally drained inside. I also run occasionally, and when I do, I find that I go too far—maybe four and a half or five miles—and then my knees hurt. Sometimes I even work out and run the same day.

"When I get compulsive in the gym is when I go in thinking I'm going to work out for an hour and then I find I went in after work at five and now it's seven-thirty. I hardly ever stay for more than two and a half hours, though. That's a long time if you work out the whole time—on the machines, running around the track, doing aerobics and lifting weights.

"For the most part I don't think there's anything wrong with it, but I have to admit that sometimes I put my exercise above everything else. For example, I have to fit my workout in before I have a date, and then I try to make it look like I haven't been working out. They don't know that I've put that first, but I've been late a lot to my apartment, where I've kept someone waiting in the lobby. I think it can be a problem because I've noticed I use working out as a way to avoid spending time with people, making dates, going to dinner and so on. Sometimes I show up at meetings halfway through or miss them altogether.

"If I miss working out, I feel sort of lost—like something's missing. Working out gives me a fabulous feeling. If I feel lousy I can go work out or I can put my headphones on and go for a run and get the adrenalin flowing and feel just great. If I have to say where the good leaves off and the bad begins as far as exercise goes, I'd have to say that it's when I use it to avoid situations and people.

"I think I really got into exercise when I was thirteen. I grew up in a family of jocks and sort of picked up the value of sports through osmosis. I got into it a bit later than the rest of them, so I think I was manic about catching up. And then my best friend died and I found that exercise was a way I could feel better without having to get that from someone else.

"But I have a neighbor, Norman, who's really an 'exercise-aholic.' He works out about eight hours a day and is always on the run. Even though he's several years younger than I am, his body seems to be a lot older than mine because he's abused it. He's got back problems, knee problems, ankle problems—you name it, and he's got it. It's because he pushes himself all the time. He'll get up at seven on the weekends and play tennis, then play eighteen holes of golf, come back and play tennis again, play basketball in the evening and then crash out totally."

DISCOVERING DAVE'S AND NORMAN'S FANTASY

Because Dave, like Noreen, had some awareness of his behavior, he knew that too much of a good thing is still too much. He also recognized his feelings—that he had a sense of being lost or adrift when he didn't work out. He knew that he sometimes used his exercise regimen as a way to avoid social situations or even intimacy.

Dave's—and Norman's—fantasy was that if they exercised enough, they would have everything under control. For them exercise was a way of whipping their bodies into shape, of keeping other people waiting, of avoiding places where intimate interchange might take place. It was an attempt to negatively control their bodies, their feelings and other people and situations.

It was interesting that Dave became heavily involved in exercise around the time of his friend's death. Even though exercise can be a cathartic, healthy way of releasing emotions, when it's taken to an extreme, as Norman continually did and Dave sometimes did, it is a way of controlling feelings and of perpetuating the unconscious fantasy that one has control over things that are in fact humanly impossible to control.

REACTIVE INSTEAD OF ACTIVE:
ARTHUR'S STORY

Arthur was a very calm, very bright, articulate man who appeared to have a perfectly normal life—to all outside observers, that is. When Arthur laughed, it was with a chuckle, not a deep, expressive belly laugh. He had difficulty with eye contact. He didn't really engage his conversational partner; rather, he tilted his head a bit to the side and kind of looked up, his eyes darting around the room. A sense of wariness and vigilance surrounded Arthur, and he appeared to be passing silent, distant judgment on those around him.

Arthur was a helping professional who lived in a nice, neat suburb with his wife and three children, his dog and his Jeep. And Arthur did what many, if not most, Americans do in the evenings for relaxation. He watched television. But unlike most other Americans, particularly other middle-aged hospital administrators, Arthur watched television for six, seven, even eight hours each evening and virtually all weekend. Arthur said he watched television to relax, but the form of television-watching he engaged in was different from that of most television-watchers. Arthur was a "grazer."

Grazers watch television with their push-button remote controls in hand, switching back and forth among at least three channels. Arthur had done so much grazing that he had worn down the button on his remote control, injuring his thumb in the process, from overuse and overstrain. For Arthur, grazing meant watching one show or film for ten or fifteen minutes until he could pretty well predict what the plot was going to be. Once he knew what was going to happen, the excitement was gone from the plot and he switched to another channel until he could predict what was going to happen on that show as well. Plot predictability has been honed to a fine art by television grazers, who have seen so much television that they've figured out virtually every plot known to humankind.

Once Arthur had figured out the plots, he started grazing only for segments of action. He moved between shows that were portraying struggles between two forces, whether cops and robbers, cowboys and Indians, the Mafia and the Chicago police force or whatever. Usually he didn't bother with love stories unless there was a major conflict between two partners that produced some sort of heated disagreement.

As Arthur flicked the remote control, he identified with the winner of the struggle in each segment of action he encountered. He could sit, passively moving from one action-packed segment to another, free of the conflicts and cares at work, king in his own living room. With a flick of the remote control he could command images to come at his beck and call. The amazing instrument at his thumb-tip could provide him with predictable heroes who always won, who were always powerful and free, unlike him.

Arthur's fascination with television was so all-consuming that if he wasn't working or actually watching television, he was thinking about it, planning it, looking forward to it. The rest of life was something to be gotten through so he could get to the most satisfying activity in his life—television grazing. Although he realized that television is a national pastime, Arthur was defensive about his compulsion. He was quite secretive about it, was defensive if questioned and recognized that it was a preoccupation with him and that he arranged the rest of his life around it. He asked his wife and children to join him in his pastime, and he wanted to put televisions in the living room, the family room, the master bedroom and each of the children's rooms. However, his wife refused.

DISCOVERING ARTHUR'S FANTASY

Unlike Noreen and Dave, when Arthur first came to see me he had almost no awareness of his compulsion, let alone the feelings beneath it or the unconscious fantasy that it betrayed. Arthur had grown up in a strictly religious home in which the expression of emotions was forbidden—not by decree, but by example. There was a sense in which only the spiritual aspect of life was acceptable; being moral and doing one's duty were the only important things in life. The body, emotions and sexuality were rejected.

In keeping with Arthur's repressive background, his body had a sense of heaviness and lifelessness about it. It was as if his body was somehow a lifeless object that he manipulated and moved through sheer force of will. His arms would lie limply on the armrests of his chair, as if they had been placed there but were about to fall off. In contrast with the lifelessness of Arthur's person, the characters on the television screen were full of life and energy, pulsating with action and vibrating with energy. Arthur, with his sense of pleasant absence, his cardboard stand-up quality, his emotional inactivity, required emotional presence and activity from another source. Television was safe: no one would get hurt in the action; Arthur's identification and passivity wouldn't cost anything—or so it seemed.

The unconscious fantasy that seemed to "have" Arthur was that he was powerful when he was watching a powerful interaction, that he was a winner when he was watching a winning interaction, that he was alive when he was watching scenes of anger, conflict and powerful confrontation between opposing forces. One of his favorite television genres was science fiction, as he loved cosmic clashes in which forces from other planets combat each other or larger-than-life cosmic beings engage each other.

Feeling our own godlike, creative powers by identifying with superhuman forces is a natural human activity, but for someone like Arthur who was never allowed to feel, who was restrained and dutiful, who never claimed his own creative potential or took forceful stands or engaged in heated disputes about anything that mattered passionately to him—for him, watching action replaced taking action.

The autonomous operation of Arthur's unconscious fantasy in his life clearly demonstrates another characteristic of an "imagined condition." It is reactive instead of active; it keeps us stuck. The "harmless" recreational pursuit Arthur lived for kept his whole life on hold. Arthur came alive only when he was watching television. The energy he put into identifying with the lives of others crippled his own and maintained his stance of passivity and reaction.

INDICATIVE OF UNDERLYING BELIEFS: SALLY'S STORY

Sally had lost three jobs in the last five years. She was a skilled legal secretary with impeccable manners and the right demeanor for an attorney's office—professional, understated, confidential. The trouble with Sally was that she was late. Incurably late. Sometimes by ten minutes, sometimes by twenty, frequently by an hour. When she came to see me she was desperate. She didn't want to be late, but she couldn't stop being late. She was ashamed, but, more than that, she was afraid she was going to lose her job. She just couldn't seem to get out of the house in the morning.

Sally changed her clothes three, four, even five times before she would leave for work. What she wore was the predominant concern of her life. But it wasn't because Sally was a fashion plate. It was because she had to have exactly the right look for each interaction of her day. If she was going to be spending time in the boss's office, then she'd need a particular look to feel competent in his presence. Lunch with a colleague would require quite another style. And then there were her moods to consider. If she was feeling calm, she definitely could not wear something red or purple.

Trying to meet all the emotional requirements of the day was too much for Sally. She became incapacitated, overwhelmed, immobilized. In my office she would recite, in agonizing detail, the clothing dilemmas of the morning. The black skirt had made her feel as if she was in a morgue, but the yellow blouse was too sunshiny for her mood today. If she contemplated wearing them together, though, the contrast would be too great; she would feel as if she were being torn apart. She thought maybe the beige suit would be a good compromise, but no, it was too drab; it made her feel washed out. Maybe if she wore her brass bracelet with the beige suit—but no, it was too heavy; it made her arm feel as if she had a thousand-pound weight on it. She wouldn't be able to hold her arm up if she wore it. She would feel weak. And she couldn't feel weak today; she had an important document to complete on that divorce suit.

DISCOVERING SALLY'S FANTASY

What I discovered was that Sally's feelings were so threatening to her that even the mention of the words "anger" or "sadness" elicited panic. All she could tolerate mention of was being "upset" or perhaps "anxious." Instead of feeling any of her feelings, Sally had unconsciously constructed an elaborate, ritualized system to express the inexpressible. Color, texture and style became Sally's emotional life. The clothing she wore had assumed the importance that her feelings should have had. Every scarf, every pair of shoes, each accessory played some part in her drama of feelings, which was projected outward because it was too dangerous to experience inside.

Sally came from a family in which her ailing 250-pound mother totally dominated the interactions of every member. There was no room in the family for anything but the mother's body, its needs, its ailments, its incessant demands. The mother pitted brother against sister and father against son, keeping the family's emotional innards stirred up, creating chaos, catching everyone off guard, turning the dissension to her own advantage. There was no place in this family for anyone else's body or anyone else's feelings. The mother was all-consuming.

In our sessions together, I worked on helping Sally to be able to identify her feelings. I'd ask her questions such as "How did you feel when you wore the blue suit to lunch with the paralegal?" Despite our efforts together, however, identifying feelings on a consistent basis proved to be too dangerous, too close for Sally to manage. It was safer to keep the feelings in the clothes, where they could be taken off and hung up in the closet, away from view. If she could have verbalized the feelings, she would have eventually been able to take them back inside herself. But our strategies didn't work, and Sally left therapy with only an ounce of awareness of her feelings and virtually no awareness of her unconscious fantasy—that if she could just find a way to create the perfect outfit for each occasion in her life, all of her feelings would be expressed through her outfits.

Sally's story demonstrates the last item on our list of characteristics of the unconscious fantasies that lie beneath compulsive behaviors and wounded feelings. The fantasies we hold—or that hold us—reveal the belief systems we came up with as a result of our early experiences. These belief systems are self-perpetuating, because even though they were created as a result of certain sets of circumstances in childhood, we take them with us and impose them on top of the other circumstances in our lives—whether they fit or not.

Sally's profound, tragic belief about her life was that there was no room for her or her feelings. She learned early on that there was room only for her mother and her mother's feelings. Her life and her feelings had to be disowned; it wasn't safe to have them. Sally couldn't seem to wake up from the family trance that had mesmerized her with its particular version of reality. Some trances are harder to wake up from than others; some require gargantuan effort, immense dedication and a monumental support system. Somehow these commodities were in short supply in Sally's life. She couldn't seem to wake up.

◇◇◇

Now that you have finished this chapter, can you identify the unconscious fantasy that is the basis of your compulsion? How would you describe it? Can you locate its roots? What role does it play in your life?

Write down your fantasy in a short paragraph, concentrating on describing it in terms of concrete details—what you see, hear, touch, taste and smell. What you learn by doing this will help you in the clarification process that will bring you one step closer to recovery from your compulsion.

CHAPTER SIX

Uncovering
Your Family Trance

A client once told me of an incident he had read about that had made a lasting impression. My client, who was struggling to uncover his own family trance, recounted the story of a teenager who opened the family medicine cabinet one day in search of some aspirin. Confronted by a set of false teeth sitting on the second shelf, she ran to her mother with the apparent evidence of a family secret. "What are these?" she asked in a puzzled tone. Giving the teeth hardly a glance, her mother hastily replied, "Oh, nothing."

Taking her mother at her word, but nevertheless feeling a bit crestfallen because her chance discovery had led nowhere, the adolescent put the teeth back in the cabinet and closed the door. "Oh, it was nothing," she mimicked. Years later when the teenager-turned-adult finally realized that indeed her mother did wear false teeth, she was confronted with a full-blown family trance. Her eyesight had told her that there was a set of false teeth in the family medicine cabinet. Her mind had deduced that if false teeth were in the family medicine cabinet, someone in the family must wear false teeth. But when her mother had matter-of-factly dismissed the possibility, she had compliantly returned the teeth to their resting place, said, "Oh, it was nothing" and closed the door. As you can see, she had been well trained to go into the family trance.

She hadn't seen those false teeth. They weren't there. They couldn't be there because they didn't fit in with the family script. Nobody wears false teeth, and her mother in particular does not wear false teeth because the family has a certain image to maintain and the teeth are not part of it. Therefore, what the adolescent had seen couldn't have been false teeth. So she rejected the reality her senses had detected and her mind had perceived in favor of a family trance.

The Family Trance

All families have some sort of group reality they subscribe to, some way of being, some system of organizing their values and interactions. As I first explained in Chapter One, this group reality and system is the family trance.

In a healthy family, the group reality or system serves and enhances the individual members, but in an unhealthy family the members are co-opted into serving the family system at their own expense. When such a family system
becomes entrenched, it eventually creates a family trance.

Today we use the word *trance* in a variety of ways. We say that hypnotists
put people into trances. We hear people who experience altered states of consciousness characterize these experiences using the term *trance*. We read about
rituals in other cultures that involve going into trances. And we may see adver-
tisements for certain New Age gurus who say they do "trance work." We even
say about a friend who is displaying dizzy behavior that he is "in a trance."

The *American Heritage Dictionary of the English Language* defines *trance*
as "a dazed state, as between sleeping and waking; stupor." The word from
which *trance* is derived, the Old French *transir*, means "to pass from life to
death." What can we discover about the term *family trance* from these
definitions?

In our opening vignette, the teenager who discovered the false teeth in the
medicine cabinet shut down her own senses and perceptions in order to col-
lude with the family perception as embodied in her mother. She literally
entered "a state of reduced sensibility" (the meaning of *stupor*) in order to
participate in the trance. She moved from a more wakeful, alert state to a com-
pliant torpor, thus avoiding a collision between her own perceptions and her
family trance.

A VERSION OF REALITY
THAT SERVES THE FAMILY SYSTEM

Eventually, the constant sacrifice of our own powers of observation on the
altar of the family system brings about some form of passage from life to death.
We cannot constantly sacrifice reality for the sake of our family's *version* of
reality without paying a price. The family trance is an approximation of reality, a version of reality that serves the needs of the family system. It does not
perpetuate the family members' living in accordance with reality; rather, it
forces them to live in denial of certain aspects of reality and causes confusion in the minds of those who have not yet been initiated into the trance,
including children with minds of their own.

Family psychologists have long noted that the most profound trance that
most of us will ever experience is the family trance. It is pervasive, continuous
and unconscious. And for many of us who are under its spell, it will last a
lifetime. The induction we receive into it is repeated over and over as we grow
up, and it is usually through hard work on ourselves, most often precipitated
by a crisis or unbearable emotional pain, that we wake up from the spell cast
over us so long ago.

It is fair to say that usually the greater the dysfunction in a family, the deeper
the trance. Not to see that father is an alcoholic, that mother is a valium addict, that the "looking good" family we are a part of is crumbling behind

its wide green lawns and its impeccable white walls requires a deep trance. What are the false teeth doing in the medicine cabinet if no one in the family owns a set?

To be caught in a family trance means that we see the world around us only in a certain way and that we interpret data only according to a certain model—despite what reality says. The facts are filtered through a lens designed to fit the family spectacles, and there's no room for anything else.

Lest I sound as if I find trances to be inherently negative, let me add that trances as an entity are not inherently positive or negative. It is the nature of the trance and its purpose that determines its worth. All of us find it pleasurable and restorative to engage in certain recreational activities that involve some form of light trance. The next time you go out on a cruise, notice the lulling effect of wind and water on the passengers. Watch how viewers are mesmerized at a tennis match. Notice how you fall into a reverie on a Sunday afternoon drive in the spring. Nature, sports, pleasant company, playful children, the music of a Galway or a Sutherland, a fine meal, satisfying lovemaking—any of these can put us into a state of being that calms our usual mental chatter and makes us feel fresh and revitalized.

LIMITING RATHER THAN EXPANSIVE

Not so the family trance. It is meant to shut us down rather than revitalize us. It is a limiting mode rather than an expansive one. It is reminiscent of the spells in fairy tales from which the princess or the knight must be awakened. Unfortunately, though, we are not awakened by a kiss, at least not by a literal one. Ours is more likely to be a rude awakening, and it can come in a variety of ways.

We have seen that compulsions are ways of avoiding feelings that are too painful to experience. We have learned that we shut down these feelings as a result of childhood experiences over which we had no control. We have discovered that our compulsions were expressions of fantasies that we unconsciously created as antidotes to our pain and as ways of making sense of our situations. In this chapter we will see how those fantasies were created as a direct result of our family trances.

Characteristics
of the Family Trance

There are five predominant characteristics that make the family trance such a powerful phenomenon:

1. The family trance limits individuals' choices by excluding information, ideas, people and things that threaten the family system.

2. The family trance uses denial to keep individual members from perceiving reality, thus perpetuating the family system's version of reality.

3. The family trance undermines the individual members' own perceptions and feelings, keeping them supportive of the family system.

4. The family trance keeps individuals stuck by having them replay the past in the present.

5. The family trance binds individuals to the roles they played in the family script.

LIMITING CHOICES: JANINE'S STORY

Janine was a jogger. Although she had started out running only a mile a day, by the time she came into therapy she was doing ten or twelve miles at a time, even though it sometimes hurt. Janine was a bright, alert, attractive thirty-year-old with a slender, toned body. She was in very good condition as a result of her exercise regimen, but when she arrived in my office, she had not had a menstrual period for several years.

Although the doctor had given Janine a clean bill of health after a complete physical, she was still worried about not menstruating. The physician had indicated that stress often plays a large role in menstrual irregularities and that probably this was the source of Janine's problem. Although she accepted her doctor's explanation, Janine was perplexed because she simply could not believe that the level of stress in her life could warrant such an extreme physical manifestation.

When Janine arrived in my office, she was troubled by two things—her menstrual pattern and her relationship pattern. She had had a series of profoundly unsatisfactory relationships with men and couldn't understand why the male of the species was so bullheaded, inconsiderate and insensitive. Although Janine did wonder, "What's the matter with me?" it never occurred to her that she might be choosing a certain type of relationship over and over, without realizing it.

The other thing that had never occurred to her was that there might be a relationship between her jogging and her menstrual problem, both physically and emotionally. Over the years I have observed a fairly consistent, predictable pattern among women who overexercise. In my experience, compulsive exercising falls into two categories, running and working out, the latter of which usually involves building body mass. The profile of the compulsive runners I have worked with involves a lot of tension and fear around being a woman. Many of these women get periods only every year or so; a number of them have severe menstrual cramps. The women who fit the compulsive runner description are usually smart, energetic, vital people. Everything they do is purposeful. They move full speed ahead. They are usually professionally successful, but with a driven quality.

Underneath the normal mask, however, there is something painful. In virtually every compulsive woman jogger I have worked with there is a consistent dynamic—that of a smart, energetic little girl who cannot slow down, who has trouble relaxing and just having fun, who can never do anything without a reason or a purpose.

Certainly when Janine came into my office, she didn't realize she was a compulsive runner. Jogging is a socially approved way of remaining fit, and it has many benefits. Janine had no idea that a basically healthy activity had turned into a driven, destructive behavior pattern; it, not she, was literally running her life. If Janine missed a day of running, she felt edgy, undisciplined, defeated. She berated herself for laziness; she feared lost muscle tone and lived in terror of fat. Like many women with this problem, Janine had a somewhat distorted body image. Her medium-built, five-foot–six-inch frame demanded more than size-six dresses, but Janine was oblivious to her tendency to gauntness.

When Janine finally became aware of the role jogging played in her life—that it ran her rather than the reverse—she could start to see that its disproportionate place in her life allowed her to ignore feelings and issues she wanted to avoid. As long as she was pounding the pavement, getting a runner's high, pushing her body to its absolute limit and feeling physical pain, her emotional pain took a back seat. Her body bore the brunt of her distress and literally acted out her stance toward life. It was not easy to face the fact that her ten-mile-a-day fix was an avoidance of crucial life issues.

In due time Janine was able to cut back on her running and start to feel some of the emotions she had masked with her compulsion. She was beset with feelings of powerlessness and lack of control. As a result of going into these feelings rather than literally running away from them, she was able, eventually, to identify the unconscious fantasy she had been entertaining for years. It was her belief, hidden even from herself, that if she could run enough, be fit enough, stick to her discipline enough, she could be powerful over and in control of her body. She could make it do whatever she wanted, and it would never become unmanageable. It wouldn't get fat, it wouldn't become slack, it wouldn't embarrass her by accumulating upper-arm cellulite or growing saddlebags. It would be strictly under control.

Overly strict control shuts systems down. And Janine's body, under such rigid treatment, had lost its spontaneity and womanliness. It had become a mere skeletal machine. No menstrual periods, an almost nonexistent bosom and a tight muscular system revealed Janine's internal need for absolute control. But what was she finally afraid of losing control over?

JANINE'S FAMILY TRANCE

The answer to this question was found in her family trance. Janine came from a nice middle-class family, a "looking good" family, clean, cheerful, hardworking, professional, successful. They played tennis on weekends, were active in local organizations and had a sense of energy and accomplishment.

Although there was a lot of conviviality, little tenderness or affection was expressed. The apparent air of equality among family members was betrayed only when the most powerful person in the family, the father, was threatened. The mother, who did a lot of volunteer work and was active in the PTA, acted a bit dizzy from time to time, but the father was a man of substance who anchored the family in a secure harbor.

Paul, the first-born, was expected to follow in his father's footsteps, attend an Ivy League college and become a professional success. Janine, who was the apple of her father's eye, was also expected to do well, to enter college and choose a suitable vocation. She was encouraged to discuss issues and express opinions—as long as she didn't diverge too widely from her father's opinions or engage him in head-on confrontations. Most of all, however, Janine was encouraged to be daddy's little girl.

Being daddy's little girl meant being prohibited from becoming a woman. A woman is sexual, has sexual feelings, is assertive and feels passionate about people and things close to her. If Janine was to remain in favor, in the role prescribed by the family script, she had to control her body. She had to avoid becoming sexual, having sexual feelings and acting in a spontaneous and passionate manner. Her constant running controlled her body, whipped it into submission, guarded it against budding sexuality, kept it where the trance told her it belonged—with daddy.

A powerful man who keeps his daughter a child and treats her as a little princess needs her to remain young and vulnerable. It is important to him that she not become a woman and escape his control. But Janine's father was not the only family member who needed Janine to remain a child. Her mother had her own, quite different, reasons for keeping her daughter from becoming a woman.

At an unadmitted level, Janine's mother was jealous of her daughter, who clearly got much more attention than she did. The daughter, who was the father's own creation, mirroring his own image, superseded the mother in importance. Because the father had trouble dealing with women as equals, he could not relate well to his own wife, who demanded more than his adoring daughter did. But even more threatening to the mother than a little girl who was preferred to her was a grown-up daughter, an adult woman. It was better for Janine to remain a child because a child was less competition for the mother.

So the family trance was heavily entrenched. Janine was not allowed to be a woman because her mother didn't want another woman in the house. And her father, who was threatened by all adult women, didn't want a woman in the house at all; he only wanted a little girl. So Janine jogged and jogged and remained a sexual child while having a lot of trouble with her male-female relationships.

Janine's story concretely illustrates the first point I made earlier about the characteristics of the family trance. Janine's role in the family script limited her in a number of ways. First, it limited her to a certain pattern in relationships with men. Janine found herself involved with a series of men, usually older than she, who at first appeared to be considerate, sensitive and interested in working on a relationship. Eventually, however, each one would invariably turn out to be overbearing, manipulative and chauvinistic. Janine was perplexed at the number of ill-tempered members of the male gender. She began to think all male-female relationships were doomed.

It never occurred to Janine, until her awareness had been cultivated, that she was in fact selecting the same type of man over and over again—a man in the mold of her father. Her expectations had been shaped by her childhood experiences; she remained dominated by the pattern until she became aware of it, began to concretely examine it and started to make choices about it.

Another limiting factor resulting from her family trance was Janine's need for everything she did to be purposeful. The control she had learned to exert to keep herself in check while playing her role from the family script made spontaneity and playfulness impossible. By clarifying the unconscious priorities and values that were governing her life, Janine was able to reject the rigidity that dominated even her hobbies, learning how to be more fun-loving and whimsical.

What limitation could be more pervasive than the unspoken command to remain infantile? To be expected not to grow from girlhood into womanhood, not to be sexual or assertive or passionate is one of the most crippling limitations a young woman can experience. From the shackles of enforced childhood, Janine finally escaped into the freedom of adulthood. Although it was not easy for her to flower into a woman when she had been forced to remain a bud, Janine became less controlling of her body, her feelings, her sexuality. Although she still feared loss of control, she put on some most attractive pounds, and she began to exercise for pleasure instead of running to avoid pain. She took up swimming and cycling, and though she continued to jog, jogging assumed a balanced place in her life.

ANOTHER EXAMPLE: LOIS'S STORY

One of the most profound and poignant examples of limitation as a result of a family trance that I have ever encountered is seen in the story of Lois, who epitomized a phenomenon I call "failing for father." Women who fail because their fathers cannot handle having powerful daughters constitute a larger percentage of the population than you might imagine. Lois, who was a brilliant young woman with a job far beneath her capability, finally decided, after a year of therapy, to apply for law school. Much to her surprise, she was accepted and began her first course with trepidation.

Neither Lois nor I could have guessed the extent of the fear she would feel at stepping out of her role in her family script. The day she got her first examination back, I found a panicked young woman seated on my office couch, test in hand, shaking like a leaf. She was afraid not because she had failed, but because she had succeeded. She had not bargained for an "A," and now that she had achieved it, her anxiety level had risen to a fever pitch. She finally had to lay the test paper down and grip a pillow. "It's okay, Lois," I said as gently as I could. "You don't have to tell your family you got an 'A.' "

The first step toward the actuality of breaking the spell she had been in all her life terrified Lois. The unwritten rule in her family, as in that of Janine, had been "Thou shalt not surpass thy father." She had been limited intellectually and professionally by her family trance, which excluded all possibility of success, fulfillment and excellence.

USING DENIAL TO PERPETUATE
THE FAMILY'S VERSION OF REALITY

The vignettes of both Janine and Lois personify the second characteristic of the family trance—the use of denial to keep individual members from perceiving reality, thus perpetuating the family system's version of reality. The "looking good" middle-class family Janine grew up in presented, to the casual observer and to the unconscious family members themselves, the picture of a healthy family. Denial doesn't have to be overt. People can demonstrate it in more insidious ways, by acting as if everything is normal and healthy when, in fact, hidden agendas exist.

The language, attitudes and behavior of Janine's family betrayed their true stance—their denial that she was coming of age, that she was becoming a sexual being. And denial is so much more destructive because in the typical family trance, it extends to include the victim of a particular dynamic. Janine, too, learned to live in denial of her sexuality. The fact was that she was becoming a woman. The fact was that she was a separate person with budding sexual energy. The family's refusal to acknowledge these facts meant that eventually Janine herself would deny her own womanhood. In the collision with reality, the family version won out—until Janine's compulsion drove her into therapy and some reality testing outside the confines of the family trance.

Lois, too, lived in a situation that denied that she was bright, competent and capable of becoming a successful attorney. The family trance's vested interest in keeping dad number one meant that Lois's innate capacities were denied existence, were never validated. Without validation, a child has neither the self-confidence nor the motivation to move to new rungs of achievement. Lois, like Janine, learned to live in accordance with her family's script, which mandated that she experience only moderate success, far below her capabilities.

Another client of mine, Alice, recalls that whenever she diverged slightly from her scripted role, her mother flashed what Alice has since learned to call the "death stare" at her. Meant to get her back in line, the stare was controlling, officious and chilling. It usually had the desired effect on Alice, who learned compliance as a way of keeping the death stare at bay. Later, in therapy, when she suddenly recalled the death stare and its impact on her childhood experience, Alice realized that she had lived in denial of this stare, never permitting herself to fully feel the emotional quality or the significance of her mother's chilling gaze. "Who wants to think her mother is giving her a look that says 'Drop dead!', " said Alice plaintively after she was able to bear the implications of her memory.

UNDERMINING AN INDIVIDUAL'S OWN PERCEPTIONS AND FEELINGS

The third characteristic of the family trance points to yet another way to keep individual family members supportive of the system. By undermining a dissenting member's own perceptions and feelings, which may be at variance with what the script says, the family trance keeps the person in line, wondering whether he or she is crazy, has got it wrong or has poor judgment.

One day one of my clients came in complaining, "I feel crazy. I just spent a weekend with my family, and they're all fine, but I feel as if I've lost my mind." We spent the next seven sessions on this uncomfortable feeling. Was Clark crazy or wasn't he? From the vantage point he had then arrived at, he understood that the disequilibrium he was thrown into upon his visit was actually a sign of his emerging well-being. But he remained tenuous in his health and did not see his family for some time.

It was very helpful for Clark to do some reality testing and to see that, despite the calm exterior, the apparent normalcy of his family, his parents and siblings were completely out of touch with their feelings, creating a rocky feeling of unreality for anyone who came in from the outside. Everyone in the family went to work, everyone functioned, everyone paid bills and ate properly, but there was no relating; all the interchanges were those of zombies on the loose. Eventually CLark could see that the extent of his disequilibrium was a measure of his growth and that one day, when he was more secure in his own reality, when he had discarded the family trance altogether, even the disequilibrium would evaporate.

By making people who do not subscribe to the trance uncomfortable, the family system manages to make itself appear to be the norm and the out-of-step individual the deviant. By creating feelings of confusion, craziness, discomfort and ineptitude, the system keeps "deviants" off balance, making them question their own judgment. With hard work, one may learn to relate to the family from his or her own position of strength, but for some people the struggle is so difficult that they opt to remove themselves from the family situation entirely, rarely having contact, if at all.

REPLAYING THE PAST IN THE PRESENT

As a child, Cassie had been the most powerful person in her family. When both of her alcoholic parents had passed out and her little brother was toddling around untended, Cassie would take matters into her own hands. She was the only functioning person in the household, and she became the caretaker by default. Often she was the only family member who could stand up and walk around, get food out of the refrigerator, take the change purse and walk to the store for bread and milk.

There wasn't much Cassie could feel good about, and her shabby clothing and unkempt hair often brought her ridicule at school. But what she could feel good about was taking care of everything at home. Maybe she was the object of derision in her classroom, but when she came home she was competent and needed. The only self-esteem Cassie had was based on taking care of things.

The way Cassie's role in the family script translated into her later life was predictable. Her caretaker role became detrimental in two major areas. First, in her job as a health care administrator, she found it difficult to delegate. She did her work, and she did it well; she found it next to impossible to assign duties to others, even though her hours were getting longer and longer and she was continuously drained. Cassie's attitude was "I can do it, and nobody else can do it as well as I can."

Because this attitude was at the core of Cassie's personality, the basis of her self-esteem, it took a long time for her to see how she unnecessarily complicated life, increased her workload, bred discontent among her subordinates and was thought of as arrogant and perfectionistic.

The second area of Cassie's life in which the family trance of the past shaped the events of the present was her personal relationships. Cassie's childhood experience told her she would not feel good unless she was taking care of someone or something. The only interpersonal role Cassie really knew how to relate from was that of caretaker. Yet people who want healthy relationships don't want to be taken care of—at least not all the time. It was only through the pain of loss—loss of both men and women friends—that Cassie was able to be shocked out of her spell and see that she was re-creating the past in the present. As long as she didn't know she was doing it, she couldn't stop it.

For Cassie, seeing the pervasiveness of her caretaking, seeing the control and the assumption that other people couldn't take care of themselves was the first step in shattering the trance. Cassie began to see that if she gave up caretaking when it was not appropriate, she could change the present. She could make choices based on reality, not on the family trance. As long as she treated her co-workers and friends as if they were her drunk parents and toddler brother, she would perpetuate the pain and emotional void of the past in the present. Cassie began to see that the present offered choices she never dreamed were available to her. The present could be a clean slate on which to write a new script rather than an instant videotape replay of the past.

BINDING INDIVIDUALS TO ROLES
FROM THE FAMILY SCRIPT

People who study family systems have observed that children are frequently placed, unconsciously in most cases, in very specific roles that are designed to serve the family structure and its needs. In her book *Another Chance: Hope and Health for the Alcoholic Family,* Sharon Wegscheider-Cruse has identified some of the most common roles: the hero, the scapegoat, the mascot and the isolate. The compulsions that drive the lives of many of my clients are directly related to the rigid roles they had to play as children and adolescents. Breaking the family spell liberates them from the iron shackles that kept them bound inside stifling, one-dimensional roles.

Cassie, the oldest child of an alcoholic family, was a classic hero. The well-being of the entire family rested on her tiny shoulders, and it was she on whom all hopes were pinned. She was born into rescuing and caretaking, into assuming responsibility and working hard. She carried the role into which she had been cast into the rest of her life—until her compulsive caretaking became the warning signal that eventually proved her salvation by putting her into so much pain that she had to break the family trance and find another way to live.

Harry, the movie binger I introduced in Chapter One, whose story will be told in more detail in Chapter Seven, was a typical scapegoat. Because his successful father and his overachieving older brother, Chris, had the family male roles all sewed up, there was no room for him to excel. When he was scouted by professional baseball organizations while he was still in high school, he was ridiculed by his brother, whose star billing was threatened by Harry's potential success. Chris even punched him in his pitching arm, precipitating a collapse of self-confidence in Harry, who never pursued his talent after that.

Janine, the compulsive jogger, played the mascot for her family. Her bright, energetic air and her cheerful compliance with and support of her parents and brother cast her in the role of family cheerleader. It wasn't until years later that the pain underneath her cheerful demeanor disrupted her performance of the mascot role, opening the space for her to give up cheerleading and get into the game.

Ron, whom we will meet in the next chapter, had a family background similar to Harry's. The youngest family member, Ron was rejected by the "boys' club" (his dad and his older brother), who golfed, fished and played tennis together, leaving Ron to be a companion to his mother and sister. The lonely youth, never included in male activities or camaraderie, learned to relate only to women who needed something. Socially, however, he was an isolate, a role that followed him into adulthood when he became a vocational counselor, relating only from a helping stance but remaining emotionally isolated, without close friends or a family of his own.

◊◊◊

Now that you have read this chapter on the family trance, can you identify your family trance? Do you know what role you played in your family script?

Uncovering the family trance that held us under its spell is only a step in the recovery process. After we learn to see that there was a family script and that we played a particular role in it, we need to break the spell, mourn the loss that accompanies the death of any person or persona and exchange the illusions that have been for the realities that can be. Breaking the spell, mourning the loss and exchanging the illusion for reality are the subjects of Chapter Seven.

CHAPTER SEVEN

Exchanging Illusion
for Reality

One of my favorite fairy tales as a child was "Sleeping Beauty." The magic of being awakened from a witch's spell by a kiss stirred my child's imagination. The marriage of Sleeping Beauty to the handsome prince—with the prospect of lifelong, idyllic happiness—filled me with excitement and wonder. The story still captivates me, for more reasons than I can name. But one reason is that I constantly see a variation on this myth in my practice.

Many people, including the clients I work with, have spent their lives under a spell. They have not been put into a long, literal sleep by an old woman with a pointed black hat, but the spell is real—and enduring—nonetheless. No handsome prince is likely to come and awaken my clients from their spell with a magic kiss. It is more likely that they will be quite rudely awakened, perhaps by a loud, shrill alarm clock. Whatever the spell-breaker, it can release the sleeper from a life of unconsciousness into consciousness, from a trance into a wakeful, active state.

Unlike the fairy tale, in which unending bliss awaits the royal couple, the lives of my clients will not be pure ecstasy after they are awakened. But they will have the opportunity, usually for the first time, to make creative, autonomous choices about how to live their lives. They will have the possibility of seeing clearly, acting confidently, choosing courageously. Their lives can be active rather than reactive—because the spell that had them in its grip has been broken and they have awakened to the light of day.

In Chapter Six we talked about uncovering the family trance that has held so many of us unwittingly captive. We listed five characteristics of the trance that can help us identify how it negatively affects our lives and looked at examples of its effects on the lives of real people. Having uncovered this trance and discovered its pervasive, formative influence, we now need to break its spell over us, mourn its loss and exchange the illusion it fostered for the reality it prohibited.

Sleeping Beauty did not fall into a dead sleep until the witch cast a spell upon her. Similarly, there was a time when most of us were awake, when we looked upon the world with a sense of wonder and possibility, when it did not occur to us that there was one right way to experience life or that there were so many limits. Of course all of us must learn that we are finite, that we are limited, that boundaries exist, and in a healthy family we learn those lessons. Those lessons help us learn who we are and where we stand in relationship to others. What we experienced when we faced life with an expectant stance was our own individual possibility.

But if we lived in a family where the system came first and individuals came second, then we began to lose our sense of possibility, of creativity. Our induction into the family trance prohibited our experiencing life firsthand, freshly, on our own terms. We learned to experience life in a second-hand sort of way, as part of a system, as an actor in a family play. The spell cast upon us when we were two or four or ten selected our version of reality for us, kept us asleep and unconscious of our own relationship to the world, to life, to others. We became sleepwalkers in a drama someone else wrote, directed and produced.

Breaking the Spell

If being under a spell was not our original and natural stance in life, then there is an alternative to being spellbound. If we can experience the "kiss" that awakens us from the spell, then we can quit sleepwalking. We can walk with the firm step of someone who is wide awake instead of the tentative gait of the sleeper. The awakening kiss that shatters the spell takes a different form for each individual.

AN ILLUSTRATION: HARRY'S STORY

Harry was dripping wet, and he was angry. He'd forgotten his umbrella, and there had been a downpour; besides that, he was exhausted. He'd been up half the night, pacing around the city, up one block and down the next, fighting the urge to succumb to the temptation to walk into a cinema. But he knew that once he sat down in the safe darkness of a movie theater, the next few days would slide into oblivion as he devoured one feature film after another.

It was entirely unfair, said Harry, that he should be wet and cold when I was comfortably dry and warm in the sanctity of my office. It was even more unfair that he had to pay to come to see me. It was bad enough to be wet and cold, bad enough to feel and resist the compulsion to stop at every movie theater in town. But to have to pay me, sitting warm and dry in my office, when *he* was the one who had all the problems . . . Harry shook his head at the lack of justice.

I agreed with him: it *was* unfair. It was unfair that he'd been so agitated that he'd had to walk the streets, it was unfair that he'd been caught in a downpour, it was unfair that he was victimized by a strange compulsion, it was unfair that he not only had a problem but had to pay to try to find a solution. And it was most unfair that I sat safe and warm and dry and relatively tranquil inside my office—and was getting paid for it!

As Harry was venting, I noticed once again a gesture that had captured my attention for some time. He was massaging his right shoulder with his left hand in a sort of gentle, kneading motion, moving his fingertips in a circular direction. "Harry," I said suddenly, "would you notice what you're doing? Just stop for a moment without moving, and stay in that position." He looked down, catching himself in the exact position I had been observing over the last several sessions. He looked up a bit sheepishly. A look of perplexity crossed his face. "What's going on?" I asked. "I don't know," he replied, laughing a bit defensively.

It was clear that Harry was completely unconscious of this mannerism and that he had no idea why he did it or what it was about. Occasionally I would point out to him that he was again massaging his shoulder, and he would again wear a look of puzzled embarrassment. Once in a while Harry would even catch himself engaging in the gesture and would give me a sideways glance to see if I had noticed. Invariably our eyes would meet, and sometimes we would burst into laughter. But we still had no clue about the origin of the mannerism.

One day I stopped Harry as his left hand was reaching up to his shoulder. "What's your shoulder saying, Harry?" I asked. We proceeded to do a little role-playing, with Harry speaking as if he were his shoulder. (This type of role-playing, in which some aspect of a person—physical, emotional or psychological—is given its own voice, is often referred to as "Gestalt work.") "I'm sore," said the shoulder. "I feel bruised. I'm aching." The unedited flow of words took Harry aback. He couldn't come up with any reason that his shoulder should hurt. He hadn't fallen. He hadn't overextended himself on the tennis court. He didn't have rheumatism or bursitis.

What Harry did have, however, was an increase in the tension in his shoulder, which now felt painfully tight and stiff. Over the next few months, by observing the gesture, by doing more Gestalt work that gave the shoulder its own voice and by working on identifying feelings, we set the stage for a breakthrough.

BREAKING HARRY'S SPELL

Finally a memory obliterated by the intervening years suddenly intruded into Harry's consciousness. Harry had been a fine pitcher on his high school baseball team—so fine that agents from professional teams had started to scout him. One day before a game Harry's older brother, Chris, had come up to him and said somewhat sarcastically, "Oh, so they're going to check you out again today?" Then he had playfully punched Harry in the right shoulder. Although it wasn't a hard blow, it was hard enough to let the younger brother know that Chris was miffed at all the attention Harry was receiving. Under the pretext of joking around, buddy-style, Harry's older brother was letting him know there would be a price for success. He was warning him, "Don't you dare surpass me in power."

It was this memory that broke the spell that had kept Harry a prisoner inside his family trance for years. Harry's father had been a successful, wealthy industrialist, and his elder son, Chris, had followed in his father's Type A footsteps. He was the star of the football team, a straight "A" student, the pride and joy of the family. In the large shadow cast by such shining lights as his father and brother, Harry had struggled constantly to find his niche. As a young boy he had played sandlot ball constantly, feeling he would never be as good a student as his brother—or the star of the football team. He knew he would never be his parents' favorite. All that was left was to go outside and play baseball.

At first Harry became a pitcher by default, but as he practiced, he began to discover that he had some natural talent. By the time he was a high school sophomore, his skill had earned him the unusual honor of being scouted at the age of sixteen. It was at this crucial juncture in his life that Harry's brother suddenly devastated him—with one jocular punch.

From that time on, Harry's pitching went downhill. It wasn't that his shoulder had been injured; on the contrary, the wound was psychological. He was being punished for affronting the family system. Gradually Harry stopped pitching. Sometimes he played only for pleasure, but eventually that stopped, too.

The loud, clear message Harry got was "You are not allowed to be powerful." What he was allowed to be was passive. He couldn't be actively involved in his own life; all he could do was watch other people be powerful in theirs—whether it was his industrialist father, his top-of-the-class brother or famous movie stars. The trance Harry was in required that he sacrifice his own talent to the family system, and the punch in the shoulder from his brother was his induction into that trance, where he remained until his shoulder pain and the memory it elicited broke the spell and awakened his consciousness.

No one wants to know that his family has used him as a sacrificial lamb. No one wants to wake up to the fact that his parents and brother have willingly, albeit unconsciously, contributed to his suffering. It is only when we are strong enough to feel the pain, vulnerable enough to embrace the message our body-mind wants to give us, that we get the wake-up kiss.   For Harry, the unconscious gesture that led to the repressed memory was the spell-breaker. The elements of his family trance and its effect on his life all began to come clear.

Instead of living with the conviction that he was a defective person with a perverse compulsion, Harry could see that his role in the family script demanded that he play a passive part. He came to understand that he was being a dutiful son—at the price of his life. When he woke up to that fact, he began to get his life back. He started to see that he had choices. He could acknowledge that there were very coherent reasons for his behavior. With his success at pitching, he had reached a place of power that was so threatening to the family system that it had to retaliate by putting him back in his place—beneath the glass ceiling he was about to break.

BECOMING AWARE OF SIGNALS

As I have said before, whenever there is something unconscious inside us trying to become conscious, whenever there is something we need to know— for our growth and good—we will get signals. Harry's signal was his gesture of massaging his shoulder. His body-mind was trying to tell him something, and he listened to the message, even though it took a long time for him to understand it. It is often the body that reveals something about the family trance, for the body may act as a picture of our unconscious, betraying things we have wished to remain unaware of.

Freudian slips may do the same thing. "Where did that come from?" we may ask as we hear ourselves utter an embarrassing "slip of the tongue." Dreams may often give us signals about something we need to look at. These signals, or clues, usually "don't make sense." My clients protest that the clues they get or the slips they make "don't fit" their conscious beliefs, attitudes or assumptions about situations in their lives. Often when I see a puzzled or sheepish look on a client's face and I ask him to tell me what he's thinking, I'll get a response of, "But it doesn't make sense." I'll counter with, "Say it, even if it doesn't make sense; say it, *especially* if it doesn't make sense— because it won't make sense anyway." The idea that things should make sense is often what we were taught growing up. It's often an old way of seeing things. Saying whatever pops up in the safety of a therapeutic relationship—or a trusted friendship—may give us the opportunity to explore the new meaning that comes from breaking old patterns of meaning. If we're ready for the kiss that breaks the spell, we will receive it—perhaps not in the time we think is best, but in the best time.

USING DRAMA TO BREAK THE SPELL: CASSIE'S STORY

Sometimes the kiss that awakens us from our spell can take a dramatic form. Cassie, whose story I introduced in the last chapter, was able to feel sad about other people, but not about herself. She was very compassionate, and if she saw someone on a city street in need, she felt devastated and invariably gave him money. Even a destitute or abused person on television could elicit tears. One day at a therapy workshop, it was Cassie's turn to re-create her childhood home through a psychodrama, a type of role-playing in which group members act out scenes from each other's families of origin, assuming the roles of parents and siblings. She saw her mother passed out on the floor, her father lurching about and her little diaper-clad brother sitting on the floor whimpering—and then she saw herself as a little girl trying to pick her mother up off the floor, trying to get her little brother something to eat. "What would you like to say to that little girl?" I asked Cassie. "Oh, that poor little girl," she whispered in a childlike voice. Then, overwhelmed with the truth, she cried, "Oh, my God, that poor little girl is me!"

All her life Cassie had been allowed to have feelings about others, but never about herself. Only when she could see her family portrayed "out there"—and herself as another child—could she realize how devastating her role as child rescuer had been. The illusion she had experienced of being the brave, competent caretaker was supplanted by the sudden shock of recognition that had been inadmissible before. She had been an abused, neglected child, and her family's need for her to be a heroine, a role she had played out, had been one more form of abuse in the string of emotional assaults she had endured. But finally the spell was broken, amid tears of pain and anger.

REENACTING YOUR ROLE
IN THE FAMILY TRANCE: RON'S STORY

Yet another way to experience the "kiss" that breaks the spell is to reenact our unconscious role in the family trance—but in a situation that reveals the role for what it is. Ron, another rescuer, so completely identified with his family role that it was ruining his health, his relationships and his professional life. Every fiber of his being was committed to being "helpful" to others. Ron had no idea of what he himself wanted or needed because he'd never exercised his wants. If he had even approached the possibility of choosing what he wanted, he would have been absolutely terrified. He was a foreigner in the land of wants and needs.

In today's psychological language, Ron would be termed a "codependent"; that is, someone who is unhealthily focused, to his or her own detriment, on the needs and behaviors of other people. One of the common characteristics of codependents, as the most widely read books point out, is the need to control, which is usually masked as helpfulness. Usually rescuers or caretakers grow up in circumstances that are so chaotic and unpredictable (either emotionally or otherwise) that their only sense of security lies in controlling the environment and the people around them. They fear that if they don't take charge, the resulting chaos will be insurmountable.

Ron was a social worker in a state agency, where he was typically overworked and underpaid. In addition to his heavy caseload, Ron often assumed responsibilities for his boss, who was not codependent and knew a workhorse when he saw one. After spending his whole day helping people, Ron would return to a private life where he helped some more. All his girlfriends and other friends were helpless, dependent people who had enormous problems that required hours of listening time.

Although Ron ended up, predictably, frantic and exhausted, the only time he ever took for himself was when he was so sick or emotionally drained that he spent the weekend in bed watching television with the shades drawn and the phone off the hook. Since Ron's only way of relating to people was by being helpful, isolating was his only alternative. Usually he emerged from his hours of isolation somewhat rested but considerably more depressed, for what he really needed was human contact that nourished him rather than depleting him.

Ron's caretaking compulsion was so pervasive that it could never have been confronted directly, the way less pervasive behaviors often can be. I had to let Ron play out his scripted role with me for a long time before his behavior itself, in the searching light of therapy, could reveal to Ron the spell he was in—and break it.

One of the issues Ron and I soon got into was who would direct the session. The idea of my directing our sessions was intolerable for Ron because if I directed, he was not in control. Ron had a major investment in appearing powerful, knowledgeable and in control, so he spent a number of sessions proving he was in charge. He would protect his territory by talking through the entire session about things *he* wanted to talk about, overriding any comments I might make, or perhaps not even hearing them. For him as a male to come and see me, a female therapist, was particularly threatening. Most of the women in Ron's life were women who either were helpless or feigned helplessness to make him appear powerful and ensure his rescuer role.

Since Ron couldn't really rescue me, because after all I was the therapist, he found ways to help me be the best therapist I could be. He was going to be the helper's helper. He might come in, for example, and sit down thoughtfully and seriously. He might express concern for me, saying that therapy is hard work. He might say I looked tired and ask if I was getting enough rest. He knew therapists work hard, and he was going to help me and take care of me.

Then he might say that he had been thinking about the last session and that I had made some really good points. It was true what I had said about his boss being so easily threatened by the way he, Ron, had handled the drug case. Then he might tell me about a particular theory he wanted to apply to the situation and help me develop that theory. "I think if we approached it this way . . . ," he would say. Or, "I think we ought to start using dreams a bit more in our sessions."

At this stage of his therapy, it was very important for me to let Ron behave this way in session so that he could feel what it was like to be the caretaker—and to have him pay for it. Here he was, driving into the city to see me from way out in the suburbs after a hard day's work; he was paying me money, and then he was taking care of me, too. "Are you overworking?" he would ask. "Is there enough heat in here?" If his session was at four in the afternoon, he might bring me a piece of cake because most people get a little drowsy at this time of day and he wanted me to have enough energy to get through all my appointments.

One day I decided the time was right to broach the subject of being helpful. "It kind of feels like we're in this together, that you're kind of helping me think about what to do during the session." Although his demeanor became a bit defensive, he agreed with me, "Yes, it does." Then a bit later, I broached the subject of his paying money to take care of me. Now money was a real issue for him, so this was a sore spot. On the one hand, it felt good to be competent enough to help the therapist, but on the other hand here he was, getting ripped off, just as he was in his other relationships, where he was taken advantage of.

After several gentle confrontations of this sort at consecutive sessions, I could detect a shift in Ron. He was beginning to lose his mask of competence, to shift around in his chair a bit. His breathing would change, and he would appear tense. There would even be a moment of silence now and then. It felt as if he was starting to allow his behavior pattern to enter his awareness. Bit by bit he began to get enough distance to examine his behavior even while he was engaged in it. In the safety of a caring therapeutic relationship, he could watch how he relived the rescuer role again and again and again. And because Ron had a good sense of humor, he was able to laugh later when he realized he was taking control of therapy again. Learning to examine his behavior and to trust me, he slowly started to relinquish his iron-clad control, the first step in breaking the spell his mother (deserted by his father) had cast upon her son, in whom she had invested the world.

CONFUSION: A STEP TOWARD CLARITY

Often around the time that clients are beginning to be painfully aware of the system that has kept them locked into particular roles, they experience a lot of confusion. Confusion often acts as a defense against knowing something we aren't quite ready to see. In the transition into recovery, confusion is an important step because it is a step toward more clarity than we had when we were stuck in the old rut, the old system. Confusion indicates that the old way of being is starting to break down, but a new orientation has not yet been formed. The reason we need confusion as part of the transition is that we are still too afraid to know the truth because it will hurt so much. Once we see it, we won't be able to "un-see" it; we'll have to change, and we're not quite ready. It's very unsettling to uncover our family trance and then to see our part in it and break the spell. Which of us wants to know that the people we've spent an entire lifetime with have been lying to us in one form or another—or keeping huge secrets from us—or have been willing for us to deny our feelings? Eventually we will be able to make our peace with that, but when we're first discovering it, it hurts.

Although confusion is a giant step down the road from denial, which allowed us to live inside the trance, thinking all the time that it was real, it is only an intermediate step. But if we don't take the next step in our growth, we can get stuck in confusion. Feelings of disequilibrium and disorientation often surface at this time of the breakdown of the old structure in our lives. The body may give signs that changes are occurring, causing confusion. Ron, for example, would shift uneasily in his chair, become agitated and unconsciously change his breathing rhythms, giving me an indication that awareness was dawning and the old mask was crumbling.

Sometimes the confusion can be deeply unsettling. One client, on her way to see me, had boarded a bus and then suddenly couldn't remember where she was going. Her first instinct was to think, "Oh, I'm going crazy!" In her case her temporary loss of memory and her feelings of being crazy were her last defense against some powerful feelings and insights that were ready to break through her usual consciousness. In this kind of situation, confusion is the gate that keeps the feelings and insights at bay; when the gate finally swings open, the awareness and the pain flood in. But temporarily my client was sure she was going crazy, that I was pushing her into insanity. Later on, she could look back and see that she had been defending against the inevitable hurt she would feel as she woke up to her family reality.

Establishing New Relationships

Once the spell has been broken, through whatever means, a person's relationships with his or her family members undergo irrevocable changes. Trying to establish new relationships in the light of the new awareness is a difficult proposition.

GETTING SOME DISTANCE

What some of my clients have found is that they need a time of no contact with their parents and siblings—if that is at all possible. How long a period is necessary depends on a variety of factors, but until the new awareness has really gotten a foothold in a person's consciousness and until strategies for dealing with the family have been created, it may be important to have a hiatus.

There are two reasons to have some distance at this juncture. One is to protect ourselves and build a place where we feel safe from manipulation. The other is to reality test. If we stay away from a family situation for a while, when we finally reenter we have a perspective and a vantage point we could never have had any other way. Partly because we've been protecting ourselves, and partly because we've achieved some distance, we can come back and see the situation and realize, "Oh, it's them and not me. This dynamic *is* really going on, and I'm not making it up." Space allows for healing, and it allows for clarity.

In addition to getting literal as well as psychological distance, we also have to learn to set limits with our families. Sometimes what this means is to be clear inside ourselves what we will and will not put up with from our parents and siblings. Other times it may mean setting outer limits, such as deciding to spend three hours instead of three days at home or staying in a nearby motel rather than in the family home.

GOING HOME AGAIN

Sometimes the internal state we create, through having worked on ourselves, is sufficient to protect us. In other situations, however, it is not enough. Before we go home again, we need to note what level of awareness we are at, what level of recovery. If we are vulnerable or this is our first time back in the situation, we may need to provide some clear structures for ourselves. We may want to take a list of phone numbers of trusted friends we can call in a crunch. Or we may want to take motivational audiocassette tapes that we can listen to when the going gets rough. Literature that inspires or encourages us may be important at this time.

One client who went home to visit her parents for the first time in a year suspected it would be rough going. She made a tape from herself to herself to play during the inevitable moments of self-doubt and devastation. When some of the old feelings started to assault her, she quietly went aside to her room, lay down on her bed and played the tape. She had gone prepared, and her preparation paid off.

Examining Our Feelings

One thing we can do when we go home again is to examine our own feelings in the home situation. Many clients discover that they start feeling "crazy." It's important to note that if we are feeling crazy in a situation like this, something crazy is really going on. The trouble is that we may know it, but no one else does. There is no one to corroborate what we see or feel—just as in childhood, when we took on the craziness in our families but thought there was something wrong with us. This dynamic is so subtle, so pervasive, that it can continue to "get" us even when we've worked on ourselves for a long time.

One of the reasons it's so important to notice our bodily sensations is that they are accurate registers of what's going on around us. Knots in the stomach, tightness in the shoulders, revelatory gestures or mannerisms (like Harry's massaging his shoulder) give us clues about something going on that we're not quite in touch with. Our bodies are sensitive devices giving us readings about our environments. But what do our minds do? "Oh, I must be crazy," they say, interpreting what they see through their layers of denial and confusion. Our bodies and minds behave like those of the teenager who found the false teeth in the medicine cabinet. Our feelings are accurate in a situation, but our minds don't want to trust the body sense, the intuition, the instinct.

Doing More Research

Going home again gives us the chance to do more research, to be in the laboratory—this time with a new hypothesis. We're familiar with feeling crazy because we didn't trust our own perceptions, but hooked into the family party line instead. If we can be in the home environment and use our being there as a way to check out our new perceptions, it will probably be a healthy and validating experience for us. But if the chaos and the dysfunction is so extreme that we are sucked right back in, then we must set strict limits for ourselves. Perhaps we can take a friend with us to act as a steady beacon and reality point for us. However, in extreme cases, where there is rampant abuse, either emotional or physical, we may have to stay away—temporarily or even permanently.

Often clients come in "feeling crazy," maintaining that their families are fine, but they are "bonkers." After hours of work together, we discover that their feelings are trustable, that actually their families are "bonkers," but that the craziness of the situation is covered over with an appearance of normalcy, of calm. Everyone goes to work on time, there is enough money, meals are served appropriately and all the appearances are intact. However, everyone in the family is totally out of touch emotionally, and the art of relating to one another is nonexistent. No wonder my clients feel crazy! By reentering the situation for a visit after having worked very hard on themselves, they are able to validate and confirm their new awareness and break their spell.

Then What?

After the spell is broken, then what? We can't spend our life in one orientation, in one system of perception, and then give it up without a sense of extreme loss. And we certainly can't go back to the way things were. Once the blinders come off, our reality is changed forever, even though we will make slips and need to do a lot of clarification. The shocks of recognition we have experienced have awakened us to a new perspective on our family's behavior, as well as our own. In many cases we have been able to clarify the accuracy of our new perceptions by returning to the family for a visit, checking out our new vantage point against the reality we see more clearly—without the family trance.

It's not easy to break the spell; some people even experience physical discomfort when their world shifts. One woman I know, who said her realizations made her "sick to my stomach," found herself experiencing nausea as she discovered that a trusted person had been consistently betraying her. Experiencing nausea at such a time in a common phenomenon. Breaking the spell shatters the world as we have known it. It can be a sickening experience.

Although there may be times when we want to go back to the way things were, to the comfort of the known, however miserable it was, we find that once we have removed the blinders, we can't really put them back on; they just don't seem to fit. Besides, we start to get some sneak previews of the benefits of breaking the spell, of gaining consciousness. Breaking the spell paves the way for growth; it opens up the world and expands our panorama. But just as we must pay for everything else we get in life, we must also pay the price our new awareness exacts. One of the prices is the pain of loss.

Mourning the Loss

I have noticed predictable patterns among clients who are mourning the loss of their old roles, their old adaptations to reality. Ron, the rescuer, encountered bouts of depression as he experienced the death of his caretaker role, which had been a very safe, respected way for him to relate to the world. As Dana gave up her seductress persona she'd literally get the shakes in a bar or nightclub. She'd have to hold onto the back of her chair or the arm of an escort to quiet her unsteadiness. Spell-breaking can have visceral effects that are similar to those one might experience when getting off drugs or alcohol, although what is being broken is an emotional rather than a physical behavior pattern.   One almost universal experience of clients at this point in their work is anger at me, the therapist. As we shall see in Patti's story later in this chapter, clients may feel that I am taking away something they've clung to their entire lives, that I am dealing them a blow, a loss. A therapist must be strong enough to accept, on behalf of the client, the inevitable, predictable anger that loss brings—until the client can come to accept the responsibility for choosing the loss rather than feeling victimized by it.

Another predictable development at this stage is a feeling of great fear. Breaking the predominant orientation we've had since childhood is like taking a pacifier away from a baby. Without the pacifier we feel acutely the fears we've hidden from ourselves—fear of the unknown, of change, of accepting responsibility, of freedom, of growing up. Giving up the roles we learned to play in our families, breaking the spell, inevitably means growing up, assuming responsibility for our own choices, becoming adults, not blaming others. Giving up these roles is tantamount to finally leaving home, even though we may have been gone for years.

Many clients, when they begin to feel the terror of giving up an old orientation without quite knowing what the new one will be (and we can't really know it ahead of time), slip back into some of the old behavior. It's pothole time. It somehow seems safer to go back than to go forward. But what happens when they go back? It's not the same any more. They know too much; they've experienced too much; they've changed too much. But these slips, these excursions into old behaviors, act as great clarifiers. They show them what they've left behind—from a new vantage point—just as visiting their families with their new consciousness tells them what it must have been like there as a child.

Sometimes clients feel like returning to their old orientations, but they are able to see that it wouldn't benefit them to do that, so they make a choice not to go back, even though they may feel like it. In Patti's story we will see how she would do what I call "thinking it through"—that is, mentally role-playing what would happen if she repeated the old behaviors. Even though we may feel fearful about giving up the old, childish orientation, we can learn at this stage that this is not childhood and that as adults we have choices available to us that we did not have available as children in our families.

A friend of mine used to tell an anecdote about a man with a small salary who had faithfully saved the money from his menial job year after year in order to take a cruise he had longed to go on. Eventually his dream was realized, and he set sail on his three-week adventure. One day, noticing that he never saw the man at meals, a shipboard acquaintance asked him where he was at mealtime. "Oh," said the man, "I didn't have enough money to pay for the cruise and the meals too." The astonished acquaintance could hardly contain himself as he explained compassionately to the man that he didn't have to eat canned food and crackers in his cabin; the meals were included in the cruise cost.

So many of us are like this unwitting cruise passenger. We carry our false assumptions, our limited attitudes, our old way of being with us into the new situations we encounter. When we break our spell and see new horizons before us, we need to be careful that we don't bring our old limitations along. We're on a new journey that has more benefits, surprises and gifts in store for us than we can imagine. But if we aren't open to accepting them, we will be living in an attitude of loss rather than gain. There is a time for experiencing the pain of loss, but we can't linger there too long. Loss is essential—but it is the door to a life that is larger than the one we had before.

From Illusion to Reality

Until we found out that we were living inside an illusion, we couldn't exchange it for a newer, larger reality. Piercing our illusions, although painful, is almost like getting to start over. Options that were not available to us before suddenly become possibilities. Discarding the old script that was written for us by someone else means being able to write our own. But it's hard work. Doing the hard work is what Part Four, *Recovery,* is about. But before we move on, Patti's story tells how one woman broke her spell, mourned her loss and exchanged illusion for reality.

AN ILLUSTRATION: PATTI'S STORY

Gambling is one of the most difficult compulsions to work with because it is so pervasive that it can invade even the smallest actions of a gambler's life. A steady series of little gambling scenarios often occupies the gambler's stream of consciousness, turning whatever is happening into a bet. An avid gambler may turn even a very ordinary conversation into a win/lose situation. "I'll bet she clears her throat three times before we get to the stoplight," a gambler may say to himself about a friend or colleague.

Although we all play little games of chance with ourselves or with others from time to time, games of chance completely dominate the orientation of a hard-core gambler. Whereas most of us will occasionally play such games with the cracks in the sidewalk or with lotto, for an avid gambler all of life is approached as a win/lose situation. The set-up of the win/lose odds provides a constant rush, a continuous diversion from paying attention to any other internal conversations, thoughts or feelings. For the gamblers I am familiar with, the diversion makes it possible for them to ignore the deep-seated feelings they have lived with their entire lives—feelings of extreme powerlessness that originated in their childhood situations, where, in fact, their powerlessness and dependency were abused.

PATTI'S COMPULSION

Patti was not a hard-core gambler, but her slot machine binges had started to take a toll on her pocketbook. Hitting the financial skids brought her into my office when her accountant suggested she start looking around for another CPA—or someone else who was willing to grapple with Patti's careening budget. Patti's compulsion centered around her outings with co-workers who all boarded a bus together every month or so for a weekend in Atlantic City. Although Patti's gambling was intermittent, it was problematic in intensity. She would usually take $200 or $300 to spend, but invariably she ended up borrowing from friends, eventually parting with $700 or $800—a lot of money on her salary as an office manager.

Although Patti was still able to meet her basic expenses, she started falling behind on charge cards and loans and had to curtail her lifestyle severely to get by. The financial shambles she was creating made her ask the inevitable question: "Should I quit going to Atlantic City?" After a particularly intense spree in which she parted with $1000, Patti was scared and anxious. The plunge from her giddy gambling heights to the penniless depths below prompted her to say, "No, I'm not going" when she was told about the next office outing.

Although Patti and I had talked earnestly about the pros and cons of her gambling excursions, the decision not to go on the next trip had been completely hers. But the attitude she had adopted was that of a stern moral judge or minister. It was as if she were telling herself, "This is bad; I shouldn't do it." She had made an intellectual decision, but her emotions were still under lock and key. Her decision had not been integrated into her whole system, partly because she was not deeply enough into the process yet. She was trying to use force on her compulsion, trying to take it by storm.

PATTI'S FEELINGS

The next time Patti arrived in my office, she was furious. Darting looks of hostility in my direction, she told me what a great time the others had had in Atlantic City, how they had played a great practical joke on one of her friends, how they had all missed her and wondered why she hadn't gone. Continuing to glance at me with looks of covert rage, Patti said she felt like a weirdo; she hadn't known what excuse to give and felt left out, as if she was losing her friends. "I'll never have fun again," she concluded, sighing resentfully. I had spoiled her fun, she said. Why couldn't she go to Atlantic

City? What was wrong with playing a few slot machines now and then? It wasn't as if she went every weekend. Everybody else went; *they* didn't have to have their fun spoiled.

As I validated Patti's feelings (something she had never experienced before), agreeing that it *did* feel as if she would never have fun again, that it *was* hard to be left out when everyone else got to go, that it *wasn't* fair that she couldn't enjoy a spree, her anger began to give way to the next stage of feeling—sadness. She started to feel the sense of alienation and abandonment that was underneath the rage. And the vulnerability that the sadness eventually brought enabled us to go more deeply into the roots of her compulsion.

BREAKING PATTI'S SPELL

As we began to move back into Patti's family situation, we talked about money in her family, how it was used, where it came from and how it was earned. We discovered that Patti had come from a very low-income family and, unlike the rest of her family, she had somehow always been able to get money fairly handily by babysitting, by waitressing, by participating in a co-op program in high school and then by getting a reasonably good job. Unlike the rest of her family in other ways, too, Patti had presented herself well, was reliable and had a fairly winning personality. Because of these differences between herself and the other members of her family, Patti had enjoyed feeling powerful and special.

Gradually Patti began to connect her history with her present circumstances. Her fantasy had been that she was powerful, special. The role she had held in the family system had fed that fantasy, making Patti seem special for doing something fairly ordinary, but something the family had difficulty doing—making money. And in what other circumstances did Patti feel powerful and special? When she was playing the machines at Atlantic City. Gambling recreated the fantasy she had come to know and love, so every time she played the machines, she participated in the fantasy once again.

But all fantasy ships eventually get wrecked on the rocks of reality. Patti found that the fantasy was only a cover; underneath the appearance of power was personal powerlessness. Patti used her fantasy to feel powerful only because the family system needed her to be—for the family's sake, not for hers. Feeling powerful was only a sensation, not a reality, just as it was only a sensation in Atlantic City. The reality was the shattered budget at home; the reality was a powerless, sad little girl. The past had created the present and motivated her compulsive gambling—until Patti broke the spell.

PATTI'S MOURNING PROCESS

When Patti came to see the integral relationship between child and adult, between past and present, she was able to involve her emotions, not her intellect alone, in her choice not to go to Atlantic City. And she was able to claim her own feelings about the situation rather than sticking them onto me. But she still had a very painful mourning process ahead of her. During Patti's mourning, she chose to isolate herself.

Choosing Isolation

Seeing that playing the slot machines was really doing her in and re-creating the past, Patti was afraid to socialize at all with her old friends and co-workers. She knew what she chose *not* to do (although she still felt like doing it sometimes), but she still didn't have anything to replace the old behavior with. She was also unwittingly reexperiencing her past before she could really let go of it. By isolating, she was acting out the reality of her childhood instead of the fantasy she had held about it. Underneath the idea Patti had needed to perpetuate of how her childhood had been lay the reality of what it really had been. Going through it again was a way of mourning, preparatory to saying goodbye.

Reexperiencing Childhood

By staying home, feeling left out, as if there was nothing to do, all alone on the weekend while everyone else was in Atlantic City, Patti experienced her childhood experiences all over again—this time with consciousness. The difference was that this time she wasn't really a child. She felt the feelings of childhood, but with the consciousness of an adult. She could feel the feelings, notice that she was feeling them, see where they came from and why she had them, and then see that she was no longer that powerless little girl. She was an adult—with choices and a potential for much greater power than she had ever laid claim to.

Patti's mournful reexperiencing of growing up in a home where there had been very few resources, where there had been few ways to feel nourished, where physical and intellectual life had been bereft of comfort and stimulation, where emotional life had been impoverished, was causing her to relive the past so she could choose a different future. Her mourning was deeply purposeful—even though she hadn't set out to make it that way. Patti's chosen distance from her friends also served to show her how deeply detrimental her compulsion had been, how it had been a reaction to her past and therefore no better. And ironically, she said, the compulsion was really the *same* as the patterns of the past.

Although not everyone reexperiences the past as part of the mourning process, it is important to remember that whatever form mourning takes, it hurts. Loss hurts; bereavement hurts; death hurts. And something real is dying here: a part of who we are—or were.

Going Home

About the time that Patti had chosen to isolate herself from her friends and co-workers by not going with them to Atlantic City, she decided to visit her family. As I mentioned earlier, returning home is usually an experience that acts as a clarification of where we have arrived in our awareness. Since this was Patti's first visit home since she had started her process, predictably she felt as if she were on an emotional rollercoaster.

Just seeing the house brought forth great feelings of sadness. It was dirty, in disrepair, with an odor throughout the rooms. Watching the interactions between family members lent support to the insights she had been gaining in therapy, to the dismemberment of her fantasy and her illusions. She saw the pain in her mother, the rage in her father, the chaos and neglect in the household. She noticed that she felt like a swimmer caught in angry currents trying to swim safely to a peaceful shore, but the more she swam the farther she was from the shore.

Patti felt an almost overpowering urge to grab the compulsion, to go to Atlantic City, to indulge the fantasy, to say the reality wasn't so. But now she was able to see more clearly than before the illusion she entertained—that this time she might win tons of money and bring it home to the family, and then everyone would be on easy street and she'd be a star.

Thinking It Through

When Patti returned from her visit and we had our next session, we entered another stage that seems to be an earmark of the mourning process—"thinking it through." Because she really felt as if she couldn't make it through this period without another trip to Atlantic City, we made a trip ourselves—a verbal trip. We went through each part of the trip together, detailing what happened on such trips, how it felt and what its effects were. Although it was difficult for Patti, on the rebound from her home environment, facing the stark family reality without her fantasy, without the compensating "high" the slot machines provided, she opted to make a trade-off. She would give up going to Atlantic City knowing she'd have $700 or $800 more in her bank account, knowing she wouldn't face her checkbook with despair.

But in order to stick to her decision, Patti had to have a life support system—and we had started working on one together before she had gone to visit her family. Such a system is important for a variety of reasons. It is a good antidote not only to home visits, but also to attacks of lethargy, boredom and cynicism that inevitably accost people learning to live without their compulsion, their fantasy, their trance. Compared to the sensations we experience in the grip of a life lived under illusion, reality can feel pretty tame at first. It feels like less-than-life.

For most people with compulsions, life is divided into two parts—life and not-life. Life is the compulsion, the sensation, the thing that makes them feel sparkly, energized, alive. Not-life is everything else. It is a way of marking time until they can engage in their compulsion again. Because the real feelings have been overlaid by the compulsion, because these feelings have been mistreated and replaced by sensation, those of us who are exchanging our old illusions for new realities need to discriminate between sensation and feeling.

Creating New Realities

During this period of mourning, we must sacrifice sensation for real feelings. Although reality seems pale in comparison to the high we used to feel, we know, through our awareness, which has been tested and retested through clarification, that we "can't go home again." So we start working on ways to create the new realities we are moving toward. For Patti, this initially involved drawing up a list of "safe" people to call and to cultivate friendships with, a list of "safe" activities and a list of all the "I can't's" that needed eventually to be changed into "I can's." After her first few "safe" outings (including a picnic, a visit to an art museum and a bicycle race), Patti said in each case she had felt as if she'd been to a funeral. This is a comment frequently made by my clients when they are first experiencing life without their compulsion.

Of course these activities will feel funereal at first. They don't have the charge of the compulsive behavior, the power of the fantasy, or the illusion of the trance. But the spell has been broken and it's too late to ignore the reality—as Patti discovered through the clarification her visit home had provided.

For Patti two other strategies worked quite well during this time of loss. One was exercising. She did this a bit compulsively, perhaps, but nevertheless her trips with the bicycle club gave her a physical outlet, a means of meeting new people and a hobby to keep her mind off the slot machines. Often people will trade in one compulsion for another, usually less pervasive one. This can be part of the mourning process that helps people who are in a great deal of pain to survive the loss of a more debilitating behavior pattern. But it is important that this be a "cooling-down," transitional part of the mourning process.

The other strategy Patti tried (and I certainly do not advocate this for everyone) was making "controlled" visits to Atlantic City. After looking at her budget and schedule to see when was a good time to go, Patti would take between $200 and $300, she would confide in two friends from work by whom she felt supported, and she would tell her colleagues they were not to loan her money in Atlantic City *under any circumstances.* Patti's careful planning paid off; her subsequent excursions were successful, resulting in her having a good time without going on a compulsive gambling spree.

Although both Patti and I had some concerns about this strategy, we felt our way along in the process, finding out what Patti's limits were and what worked best for her. As Patti's trust in her recovery process grew, she became increasingly confident that the more new realities she created for herself, the more the old, punctured illusions would recede into the background.

◇◇◇

Now that you have discovered your unconscious fantasy, uncovered your family trance and exchanged illusion for reality, you are ready to go on to the final stage in the process represented by this book: recovery.

PART FOUR

Recovery

CHAPTER EIGHT

Assessing
Your Needs

In Part One, *Irresistible Impulses, Irrational Acts,* we discovered how compulsions act as mood-altering behaviors that have destructive effects on our lives. In Part Two, *Awareness,* we learned how to discover whether a compulsion was interfering with our lives, how to become aware of the cycle and pattern of a compulsion, and how to identify the feelings that lie hidden underneath the cover of a compulsion.

In Part Three, *Clarification,* we discovered that a compulsion pointed to the existence of an unconscious fantasy we were continuously trying to realize by reenacting the compulsive behavior. We also traced the fantasy to its origins in the family trance, which assigned us a particular role to play in the family system. We learned that, by breaking the spell of the trance and mourning its loss, we could choose to act freely rather than according to unspoken family rules and could trade in an illusion-based life for a reality-based one.

Now that we have become aware of our compulsive behavior patterns, have clarified their source and their reason for being and have seen that our awareness brings choices we did not think we had, we find ourselves ready for Part Four, *Recovery.* Part Four is about the actual process of moving from an illusion-based life to a reality-based one as we become increasingly free of the old compulsions, behavior patterns, dictatorial feelings, fantasies, family trances and old scripts.

No matter how miserable we may have been, no matter how unhealthy our behavior patterns, we were familiar with the old way of being because we had so much practice at it. Moving toward healthy patterns can be terrifying, awakening our fear of the unknown. Without the old constrictions, our world opens up; it feels larger, more spacious. It presents more choices, requires more responsibilities and offers more challenges. How shall we cope with the new role when the old script has been torn up? Part Four offers help with this task.

First, before destructive old patterns can be replaced with healthy new ones, we must take inventory. In this chapter we will make a realistic assessment of our physical, emotional and spiritual needs so that we can create a more balanced, complete life, responding constructively to our legitimate needs rather than destructively, as we did when our compulsions drove us.

Once we have assessed our needs—probably for the first time—we can begin to create new reality-based life patterns to respond to these needs. Chapters Nine and Ten offer practical guidelines on how to provide ourselves with physical, emotional and spiritual nourishment.

When we have assessed our needs realistically and planned strategies to ensure that we meet most of them most of the time, we will need to find some way of maintaining our healthy new life patterns. A support system is essential if we are to build a strong foundation for continuing personal growth and change. Chapter Ten will detail the elements necessary for a strong support system.

It is important for us to remember that the process of awareness and clarification we have been through has brought us to the recovery stage where we are now. But the process of awareness, clarification and recovery is not a static, linear process that is completed once and for all. As researchers are increasingly discovering, growth comes from disequilibrium, which is the natural state of all life. It is the effort to create balance out of imbalance, order out of chaos, harmony out of disharmony (in both the physical and the psychological realms) that causes life, both human and nonhuman, to evolve toward ever-higher levels of development and consciousness.

Similarly, the process of awareness, clarification and recovery is continuous, cyclical, like a spiral. Even though we shed our compulsive behaviors and find healthy ways to meet our needs, there will always be some aspects of our lives that call for more awareness, more clarification, more creative life patterns. We are not so different in one way from our reptilian friends, the snakes; the skins we shed aren't quite as visible as theirs, but our molting process is real nonetheless.

ADMITTING YOUR NEEDS

Many of us grew up in circumstances that have prevented us from admitting that we have needs. Having needs somehow seems equivalent to being "needy," which carries connotations of impoverishment, of being incompetent or inferior. Our culture in general is hard on people who have needs, too. It is best not to have needs. But if we do, we are supposed to get them met with as little noise as possible. If we can't get them met, we should ignore them; they might go away.

Ignoring needs or being secretive about them creates a perfect breeding ground for compulsions, which become surrogate ways of meeting needs— ways that, as we have seen, don't work for us, but rather work against us. As the case histories we have seen so graphically point out, compulsions are the result of misplaced, displaced needs. Compulsions interfere with our ability to perceive and meet our legitimate needs; they divert our attention so we don't know that we have needs, and then they keep us from meeting them.

THE IMPORTANCE OF HAVING OUR NEEDS MET

In recovering from compulsive behavior patterns and planning strategies to develop healthy patterns, a crucial, practical first step is to take a needs inventory. Before taking such an inventory, it is important to remember that all human beings go through a natural progression of developmental stages from birth to death that is characterized by increasingly sophisticated levels of needs. Not having a basic need met impairs our ability to have later, more complex needs met satisfactorily.

For example, a newborn baby learns, in the first year of life, whether it is safe to trust the environment. Will someone feed her? Will she be held and cuddled? If a baby learns to trust that her basic needs will be met by the environment around her, she will approach the succeeding developmental challenges with more confidence and security. As an adolescent, she will be able to concentrate on such developmental tasks as becoming competent in certain skills. Her concentration on skills will be supported by the fact that other more basic needs have already been met, allowing her to approach the world with a realistic degree of trust and expectation.

Compulsions as Responses to Unmet Needs

No family or set of circumstances can meet every child's needs perfectly, but a healthy family meets most normal needs fairly adequately. However, if we were raised in circumstances in which most of our needs were not met at all or a particular need was met insufficiently, our response to life as adults will not be as confident or competent as it might have been. The areas in which we are lacking, unable to peak developmentally, are the areas in which compulsions may be expected to rush in and fill the void. Our insecurity, our inability to cope with certain situations, may cause us to grab onto a negative behavior pattern the way some people reach for alcohol and other drugs.

The compulsions we have as adults may also point to the age or stage we were at when specific developmental needs were not met. Thus we may experience arrested development until we revisit the tasks of the stage we were at when our needs went begging. An inventory can help us go back and assess the gaps in our developmental progression, as well as other needs we may be unaware of. It can also help us assess which needs we can realistically expect to have met, either by ourselves or by others.

Powerlessness: The Root of Compulsions

The most crucial issue having to do with needs assessment is power—or powerlessness. At any point and in any situation in which our needs were not met, we experienced a sense of powerlessness. In my opinion, it is from this sense of powerlessness, which can arise at any stage of development as a result of any unmet need, that compulsions spring.

During his first year of life, a child *is* powerless to meet his own needs. A newborn cannot go out and get what he wants; he must depend on other people to feed, clothe and shelter him. Nor can he coerce others to care for him. He is completely at his caretaker's mercy. As we have mentioned previously, the difference between then and now is the difference between childhood and adulthood. Although we may still *feel* like children, we are *not* children. We have the power to meet many of our own needs—or to get them met by others. And those we cannot meet or get met, we have the power to consciously relinquish.

In taking inventory, we can put the words of the now-famous "Serenity Prayer" to good use. We can "accept the things we cannot change" by accepting the fact that some of our needs cannot realistically be met; we can "change the things we can" by deciding on the appropriate action to take to get those needs met; and we can "know the difference" by making a careful assessment of what our needs are, whether they are currently being met and whether (and by whom or what) we can realistically expect to get them met.

Just seeing the difference between what was then and what is now is the first step toward claiming legitimate power that enables us to break our enslavement to the past and to the compulsions that it spawned. Knowing what we are powerless over is also powerful; it lets us work on what we can change and relinquish what we can't—or choose not to—change, as the "Serenity Prayer" and all the twelve-step programs advise. Identifying our needs, choosing the actions necessary to meet them and finally meeting those needs makes us powerful. It makes us responsible for our own lives and generates an ever-deepening sense of autonomy and self-esteem. As we meet our needs, we identify new levels of adult needs, choose new actions and meet our new needs. The cycle continues to deepen and broaden us as we claim more and more internal power, as we waste less and less time trying to change other people, other circumstances, other things.

Then, ironically, we will note that because we have claimed legitimate power (that is, control over our own lives) and relinquished illegitimate power (that is, attempts to get what we want through manipulation and control of others), things outside ourselves have changed anyway. The positive change that comes from meeting our own needs and our own goals brings such self-esteem, serenity and autonomy that our positive attitude naturally flows out toward others, who sense our inner power. Because we know how to care for ourselves, we can care more naturally for others without trying so hard. Because we are not in a state of depletion, because we are not powerless or deprived or impoverished, because we have confidence in our ability to provide for ourselves, we can respond appropriately to others. And because we are living in accordance with reality, we can set limits and boundaries where we need to, protecting ourselves appropriately from people, places and things that erode our self-confidence, damage our autonomy, and destroy our serenity.

Assessing Your Physical, Emotional and Spiritual Needs

In assessing our needs, it is helpful to break our inventory down into three main areas—*physical, emotional* and *spiritual*. Because compulsions are driven by unmet needs in any and all of these categories, a complete inventory will help us take stock of areas in which abuse or neglect have impaired our health and well-being. If we are unclear about whether our needs are being met, it may be helpful in our assessment to ask ourselves four sets of questions I have often used in working with my clients. If, for example, we are trying to assess how well our needs in the area of physical exercise are being met, we can ask ourselves the following four sets of questions concerning the quantity, quality, frequency and variety of exercise we need:

1. What is the quantity of exercise I need? What is the quantity of exercise I currently get?

2. What is the quality of exercise I need? What is the quality of exercise I currently get?

3. What is the frequency of exercise I need? What is the frequency of exercise I currently get?

4. What is the variety of exercise I need? What is the variety of exercise I currently get?

Applying these questions to all our needs, whether they are physical, emotional or spiritual, will help us draw a fairly specific profile of what our needs are and whether they are being adequately met. They can help us determine whether we are achieving balance in a specific area of our lives, in this case exercise. In assessing the quantity of our exercise, we may discover we are getting no exercise at all. Or we may be abusing our bodies with too much exercise, like compulsive exercisers Dave and Norman, who are discussed in Chapter Five. Assessment of the quality of our exercise may show us that we are exercising enough hours a week, but we are building muscle mass and not getting any cardiovascular benefit. Looking at the frequency of our exercise shows us how we space it—whether we are exercising regularly enough or are going on exercise binges that are not evenly enough spaced to keep our bodies healthy.

Assessing the variety of our exercise helps us to determine whether we are adopting a rigid attitude toward our exercise routine, acting like drill sergeants toward our bodies, which crave different kinds of movement according to weather, season, mood, tension and a host of other factors. If we are forcing ourselves to do 150 situps in fifteen minutes every day, no matter how we feel, we are taking a rigid, unnatural attitude toward our bodies. Such an attitude is in itself compulsive, resulting in a lack of spontaneity and balance, the very qualities we benefit from.

In taking inventory, we need to notice the connotations we attach to the words we use to name our need categories. Unfortunately, the word *exercise* has come to carry connotations of force, punishment, rigidity and pressure. For many people it has lost its quality of playfulness, fun, spontaneity and camaraderie. Your inventory can help you notice what attitude you are adopting toward categories of physical needs such as food, sex and touch, as well as exercise.

ASSESSING YOUR PHYSICAL NEEDS

Unfortunately, the rigidity that so many of my clients—and so many people in our culture—apply to areas of bodily need such as exercise and food indicates a widespread negative attitude we have toward the body. I have seen this attitude result in a host of deep-seated compulsive behaviors. Commonly called the mind/body split, this attitude is reflected in an amusing, yet poignant, satirical vignette in a film entitled *The Adventures of Baron Munchausen*. The vignette portrays a king who lives in a perpetual state of war between his body and his head, which floats around making intellectual and moral pronouncements. The body, meanwhile, runs about like a savage beast, wanting more food, more sex—more, more, more. The disdain of the mind for the body epitomizes the split that keeps the two antagonistic, violating the wholeness of our human need.

We sometimes forget that we are a whole system, and, as I learned so well from my mentor, Ilana Rubenfeld, subjugating the body to the mind throws the whole system off. (Ilana Rubenfeld is a pioneer in mind/body work and the creator of the Rubenfeld Method, a process that allows one to contact, express and work through body tensions and stored emotions by using touch and subtle movements.)

The Mind/Body Split: Rita's Story

One of the most unusual compulsions I have ever worked with was a direct result of the mind/body split, of one client's deprivation in the area of her physical needs. Rita was a lovely young woman, appealing, vulnerable and physically attractive. Although relationships literally came to her without any effort on her part, the men she became involved with inevitably proved to be insubstantial, unreliable and unavailable for any kind of committed relationship.

Typically Rita would be approached in a coffee house, a bookstore or even a conference or a retreat center by a young man who appeared to be sensitive, artistic, vaguely bohemian. He couldn't believe it, he'd say; he had seen her face in a dream last night, and here she was, in person. What was her astrological sign? Did she have Libra rising? Had she been to this meditation center before? And the rose quartz she was wearing—it was identical to the one he put under his pillow each night to ensure peaceful dreams.

Of course Rita would be drawn in; she would feel flattered and touched by the hand of destiny. The young man was sincere—and earnest. Convinced that she had finally found her soul mate, Rita would fall into a magical, trancelike, all-consuming relationship that included, she would confide, a sensational sex life. It wouldn't take long for Rita to find out, however, that the young man didn't have steady employment and could never take her out to dinner. Or she would accidentally find a letter he had written to another soul mate who also seemed to enjoy a magical, transporting relationship with the man Rita had thought was hers.

It took a string of similar men and many hours of work on herself for Rita to see that her predictable relationship pattern always involved men who were not grounded in the here and now, who somehow transported her into a realm of unearthly bliss. Certainly healthy and satisfying sexual relationships include ecstatic experiences, but they are also planted in the real world. However, Rita lived in an ethereal never-never land where dreams never materialized.

At the root of Rita's compulsion were unmet physical needs. Rita had been the younger of two children. Her older sister, Pamela, had been considered the mature, sophisticated beauty of the family, while Rita had been considered the clumsy baby, mired in the messiness of childhood, with its spilled milk, strewn-about toys, soiled clothing and scraped kneecaps. In comparison to her perfect, well-groomed sister, Rita had always felt awkward, dirty, out of control. The sister, although not more beautiful than Rita herself, was considered more ladylike, somehow of higher value than Rita, with her stumbling, clumsy baby body.

The effect the family orientation had upon Rita could be seen directly in her carriage and bearing. Her movements had an element of heaviness, as if she were dragging along a heavy sack of potatoes she couldn't quite manage. Her steps were somehow unsure, as if she couldn't tell whether the sack would swing to the left or to the right. Rita gave the impression that she wasn't totally located in her body, that perhaps she was really somewhere else.

It was predictable that Rita would become involved with men who had an ethereal, other-worldly quality. Because her body, the earthly, was dirty and messy, in order to experience anything physical, Rita had to have it lifted to a higher plane. Sexuality had to be magical, transporting. The only way to meet ordinary physical needs was to pretend they weren't ordinary or physical, but extraordinary and spiritual. While ecstatic experiences are part of satisfying relationships, they do not deny the body; rather, they embrace it. When Rita could acknowledge her real, earthly needs, she could finally be realistic in deciding what avenues she could explore to meet those needs.

The Body's Wisdom

Just as Rita's mind/body split and unmet needs were acted out in her repetitive episodes with unreliable men, so we often make our bodies bear the brunt of issues we won't face up to. Sometimes a physician will refer a client whose physical malady seems to have no locatable source. The diagnosis has perhaps been tension or stress. Although our culture increasingly recognizes that anxiety causes real physical ailments, we still operate at a minimal level of awareness on this issue. Perhaps the cause of our problem is stress, but that diagnosis is insufficient to heal our malady. Stress about what? Tension where? We need to listen to our bodies and locate the source of our distress.

I once worked with a client who had been referred to me because of chronic bronchitis. We were able to trace her illness to its very real origins—having no voice in her family. A common ailment among many clients is chest pains, usually caused by the constrictions they felt when they weren't allowed to take up space in their families. Our bodies act as barometers of our internal state and often unwittingly bear the brunt of our psychic wounds. No wonder they break down under the burden. We saddle them with responsibilities they cannot bear and then castigate them for telling the truth about our unmet needs.

If we would tune in and listen, our bodies could tell us what we need to know to meet our physical needs. One area in which our culture is particularly guilty of disregard for the body's wisdom is the area of food. A nation whose best-seller book lists almost always include one or more diet books, where losing weight is the subject of a disproportionate number of conversations, has a massive problem with food. One reason for the problem is that we have a lot of fear around loss of control with food. We perceive our bodies as uncontrollable, subhuman objects to be feared, subjugated and managed. Instead of listening to our bodies' wisdom, instead of slowing down and noticing how our stomachs respond to three eggs and a side of bacon or how noisy our intestines are after that fourth cup of coffee, we keep shoveling the fuel into the furnace, appeasing our physical selves, so we can go on to more important things.

We can see how culturally acceptable it is to make our bodies "act out" our emotions and attitudes when we look at the way self-abuse is honored among "masculine" men. "Real men" are often portrayed as heavy drinkers, smokers, devourers of massive helpings of heavy food and heroes in the warriors' arenas of boxing, race-car driving and other often dangerous forms of recreation. The more we act out our psychological orientations through our bodies, the more we increase the physical needs that are likely to result in compulsive behaviors.

Another area of physical need we tend to disregard is sleep. A recent article in the *New York Times* entitled "USA: Land of the Drowsy" noted that most of us need more sleep than we realize. Instead of listening to what our bodies tell us, we force arbitrary schedules on them, keeping them going through force of will. Some questions we can ask ourselves to assess our needs in this area include these: Can I wake up without an alarm? Can I take a nap without an alarm? Can I have a productive day without drinking ten cups of coffee to stay awake? If you answer "Yes" to these questions you are probably living in harmony with your body's needs, while if you answer "No" you may be somewhat out of step with your natural physical rhythms. Sleep deprivation is a subtle form of physical abuse, one that is culturally approved. If a toddler whines or fusses, we put him down for a nap. If our bodies protest that they want a rest, we feed them some caffeine and make them go on. A baby who kicks and screams when she is hungry or sleepy or needs changing is being honest about her physical needs; she is in tune. We could learn something about meeting our physical needs by watching a small child and then tuning into our own body wisdom.

The Need for Touch

Another area of physical need that is frequently discounted is the need for touch. It is well known among health-care professionals and child-care workers that children and hospital patients who receive the best of care but little or no human touch show signs of deprivation.

One of the most poignant stories I have ever heard validates these findings. A middle-aged professional man was found to have a bizarre compulsion: Every so often he would rent a motel room and tape up his body with package tape. This embarrassing behavior pattern was eventually traced to extreme touch deprivation. Although as a child the man had not been beaten or overtly abused, he had received virtually no touch or other emotional attention. One day in kindergarten his teacher had taken him onto her lap to tape his mouth shut, as he was an incorrigible chatterbox. Even though the teacher was abusing him by taping his mouth shut, the ecstatic feeling of being held and touched was so powerful for the child that he eventually repeated the teacher's behavior, attempting to feel the same sensations he had felt as a five-year-old. The story points to a fact psychologists have come to acknowledge: When human beings cannot get caring touch, they will choose abusive touch over no touch at all.

Another poignant story that illustrates the importance of touch is that of Melissa, who grew up on a farm in the Midwest, one of several children in a hard-working, no-nonsense family. Although her other physical needs were adequately met, Melissa did not receive overt affection or touch from either parents or siblings. The rules in the household were rigid, and bedtime, with lights out, came at eight each evening, with no exceptions. Occasionally Melissa would awaken in the night, frightened by a nightmare or a thunderstorm or just feeling lonely. One night she felt so afraid that she stealthily climbed out of bed, opened her window and let herself down into the farmyard.

Making a beeline for the doghouse, she curled up with her pet German shepherd, her little body warmed by the great bulk of the guard dog. Melissa would sleep fitfully, aware of how severe her punishment would be if she were found missing from her room at dawn. But her need for physical warmth and comfort outweighed her fear of punishment, and the child spent many nights in the farmyard. Years later, as my client, Melissa recalled this childhood pattern as she struggled with her compulsion to pick up men in bars, men she had nothing in common with intellectually or socially but whose big, comfortable bodies offered her the same animal warmth she had found so sustaining as a lonely child.

Needs and Variations

In addition to needing food, exercise, sex, sleep and touch, we also need to remember our need for other basics, such as shelter, clothing, appropriate temperature ranges, movement (as opposed to mere exercise), space and adequate financial resources. If we assess our housing, for example, do we find that we have a space of our own? Is there noise pollution in our environment? Is there sufficient light and air circulation? All of these belong on a needs inventory. But the importance of individual differences cannot be overemphasized. What is a need for one person may be irrelevant to another. There are infinite variations in needs and ways to meet them.

One of the best examples of variation I have encountered surfaced with a couple who came to me about their sex life. It seemed that Barbara came alive sexually only in the spring, when buds were sprouting, birds were chirping and temperatures were rising. For her husband, Bob, who had a steadier sexual need, his wife's seasonal sexual vitality presented a problem. By being willing to assess their individual needs, state them and work out a compromise, Barbara and Bob were eventually able to meet both their own and each other's sexual needs. Although Barbara is now available to her husband throughout the year, she no longer feels guilty about her less-than-enthusiastic sexual appetite during the fall and winter, while Bob now realizes that Barbara's seasonal variations are no reflection on him personally. But he looks forward with considerable anticipation to the appearance of the first robin in his back yard! If the couple had not been willing to assess their needs together and then work out a plan to meet them, they would still be at sexual odds with each other.

ASSESSING YOUR EMOTIONAL NEEDS

The majority of clients I've worked with have had compulsions that were driven by unmet needs in the emotional area of their lives. Darcy, the people-eater, tried to meet her needs for friendship and intimacy by closing in possessively on new acquaintances; Mike attempted to establish some warm human connections by surreptitiously following acquaintances around the city; and Vanessa, the charger/spender, sought to meet her needs for professional esteem and validation by charging new outfits at department stores. Harry's unmet needs for success and recognition resulted in his movie binging; Charlotte's need for intellectual validation drove her to be compulsively fastidious about "looking smart"; and Patti tried to surmount her personal powerlessness by becoming a slot machine queen in the hope of winning power and prestige at the casinos.

Our emotional needs can be identified according to three basic areas of our lives: *work, love* and *play.* Before we can identify specific needs in each area, however, we need to define what work, love and play mean to us individually. What connotations do we attach to these categories, and how do those connotations affect our assessment of our needs in each area? Is work merely a means to a paycheck, or is it a source of satisfaction, creation and service? Does our work leave us feeling depleted or replenished? Do we want a constant challenge in our work, or do we need routine predictability? Do we prefer working with people, ideas or things? Does our work bring us enough financial reward to maintain a lifestyle that meets our needs?

What does love mean to us? Do we include in our definition friendship, familial love, sexual love and altruistic concern for others? Are we aware of our need for intimate, give-and-take relationships? Does our self-esteem come from both self-love and from the love of trusted friends and family members?

The area of play is problematic for many of us who are driven to succeed or acquire and feel that play is childish at best and a waste of time at worst. But without play in our lives, we lose our sense of wonder and childlike curiosity, our ability to try on roles, to laugh, to experience spontaneity and abandonment, to take emotional risks, to try something different. Many of us have never learned to be spontaneous or playful, and this deprivation causes us to engage in unhealthy forms of recreation. Our serious, work-oriented culture splits play off from the rest of life, causing unnatural separations that result in giving play a bad reputation. The terms *playgirl* and *playboy* carry heavily sexual, hedonistic connotations that exclude their association with pure joy and spontaneity. "Playing around" and "playing the field" are stereotypical expressions that have to do with only one side of the area of playfulness.

In this area, as in others, we would do well to slow down, notice what it feels like to be playful, observe children at play and watch what we gravitate toward in our "free time"—if we have any. Many of us are uncomfortable with free, unstructured time and have no idea how to be playful. In our needs assessment we need to notice whether we make room for unstructured time in our schedules and, if so, what we do with that time and how we feel about it.

ASSESSING YOUR SPIRITUAL NEEDS

Identifying our spiritual needs is probably the most highly individual, variable task of all. What spirituality means to one person will differ vastly from what it means to another. A "Higher Power" meets the needs of some people, particularly those who attend twelve-step programs. Others find they need the support, inspiration and community that a particular church or synagogue gives them. Specific forms of meditation or chanting provide serenity and calm for some practitioners.

Many people these days keep journals, writing down their dreams and reflecting on their insights. Still others find their inner wellsprings fed by being out in nature, taking quiet walks, going fishing and spending time in the mountains. The majesty and beauty of the natural world feed their souls. People with a more intellectual bent may find solace and inspiration in the writings of great spiritual masters whose wisdom offers sound guidance no matter how long ago they put pen to paper.

Only you can identify your spiritual needs and then assess whether you are meeting them and, if not, how you might proceed to find sustenance and replenishment.

Needs Assessment

If you will take the time to carefully fill in the following worksheets, you will be surprised at what you will discover. You will have the opportunity to do the following:

1. Identify your physical, emotional and spiritual needs.

2. Determine whether your needs are currently being met and, if so, how they are being met.

3. Determine how your needs may be met if they are not currently being met.

If you have trouble identifying any of your needs, try asking yourself the four sets of questions I use with my clients. (See page 111.)

PHYSICAL NEEDS ASSESSMENT

Fill in the blanks under each item below, noting whether that need is adequately met, inadequately met or unmet. If it is adequately met, how is it met and by whom or what? If it is inadequately met or not met at all, what would it take to meet it and what first step could you take to get it met?

FOOD

Need met _____

How and by whom or what?

_____

_____

Need inadequately met _____ or unmet _____

What would it take to meet it?

_____

_____

What is the first step toward getting it met?

_____

SHELTER/HOUSING

Need met _____

How and by whom or what?

_____

_____

Need inadequately met _____ or unmet _____

What would it take to meet it?

_____

_____

What is the first step toward getting it met?

_____

CLOTHING

Need met _____

How and by whom or what?

_____

_____

Need inadequately met _____ or unmet _____

What would it take to meet it?

_____

_____

What is the first step toward getting it met?

_____

SEX

Need met _____

How and by whom or what?

_____

_____

Need inadequately met _____ or unmet _____

What would it take to meet it?

_____

_____

What is the first step toward getting it met?

_____

TOUCH

Need met _____

How and by whom or what?

_____

_____

Need inadequately met _____ or unmet _____

What would it take to meet it?

_____

_____

What is the first step toward getting it met?

_____

EXERCISE

Need met _____

How and by whom or what?

_____

_____

Need inadequately met _____ or unmet _____

What would it take to meet it?

_____

_____

What is the first step toward getting it met?

_____

FINANCIAL RESOURCES

Need met _____

How and by whom or what?

_____

_____

Need inadequately met _____ or unmet _____

What would it take to meet it?

_____

_____

What is the first step toward getting it met?

_____

OTHER

Need met _____

How and by whom or what?

_____

_____

Need inadequately met _____ or unmet _____

What would it take to meet it?

_____

_____

What is the first step toward getting it met?

_____

EMOTIONAL NEEDS ASSESSMENT

What are your needs in the areas of work, love and play? For each of these categories, list below at least five needs that must be fulfilled for you to experience satisfaction. After you have made your list, answer the following questions in the blanks provided: Is that need adequately met, inadequately met or unmet? If it is adequately met, how is it met and by whom or what? If it is inadequately met or not met at all, what would it take to meet it and what first step could you take to get it met?

WORK

1._____

Need met _____

How and by whom or what?

_____

_____

Need inadequately met _____ or unmet _____

What would it take to meet it?

_____

_____

What is the first step toward getting it met?

_____

2._____

Need met _____

How and by whom or what?

_____

_____

Need inadequately met _____ or unmet _____

What would it take to meet it?

_____

_____

What is the first step toward getting it met?

_____

3._____

Need met _____

How and by whom or what?

_____

_____

Need inadequately met _____ or unmet _____

What would it take to meet it?

_____

_____

What is the first step toward getting it met?

_____

4._____

Need met _____

How and by whom or what?

_____

_____

Need inadequately met _____ or unmet _____

What would it take to meet it?

_____

_____

What is the first step toward getting it met?

_____

5._____

Need met _____

How and by whom or what?

_____

_____

Need inadequately met _____ or unmet _____

What would it take to meet it?

_____

_____

What is the first step toward getting it met?

_____

LOVE

1._____

Need met _____

How and by whom or what?

_____

_____

Need inadequately met _____ or unmet _____

What would it take to meet it?

_____

_____

What is the first step toward getting it met?

_____

2._____

Need met _____

How and by whom or what?

_____

_____

Need inadequately met _____ or unmet _____

What would it take to meet it?

_____

_____

What is the first step toward getting it met?

_____

3._____

Need met _____

How and by whom or what?

_____

_____

Need inadequately met _____ or unmet _____

What would it take to meet it?

_____

_____

What is the first step toward getting it met?

_____

4._____

Need met _____

How and by whom or what?

_____

_____

Need inadequately met _____ or unmet _____

What would it take to meet it?

_____

_____

What is the first step toward getting it met?

_____

5._____

Need met _____

How and by whom or what?

_____

_____

Need inadequately met _____ or unmet _____

What would it take to meet it?

_____

_____

What is the first step toward getting it met?

_____

PLAY

1._____

Need met _____

How and by whom or what?

_____

_____

Need inadequately met _____ or unmet _____

What would it take to meet it?

_____

_____

What is the first step toward getting it met?

_____

2._____

Need met _____

How and by whom or what?

_____

_____

Need inadequately met _____ or unmet _____

What would it take to meet it?

_____

_____

What is the first step toward getting it met?

_____

3._____

Need met _____

How and by whom or what?

_____

_____

Need inadequately met _____ or unmet _____

What would it take to meet it?

_____

_____

What is the first step toward getting it met?

_____

4._____

Need met _____

How and by whom or what?

_____

_____

Need inadequately met _____ or unmet _____

What would it take to meet it?

_____

_____

What is the first step toward getting it met?

_____

5._____

Need met _____

How and by whom or what?

_____

_____

Need inadequately met _____ or unmet _____

What would it take to meet it?

_____

_____

What is the first step toward getting it met?

_____

SPIRITUAL NEEDS ASSESSMENT

Put a check mark next to each item in the list below that you consider essential to meeting your spiritual needs. Then, in the spaces below each item, answer the following questions: Is that need adequately met, inadequately met or unmet? If it is adequately met, how is it met and by whom or what? If it is inadequately met or not met at all, what would it take to meet it and what first step could you take to get it met?

PRAYER_____

Need met _____

How and by whom or what?

_____

_____

Need inadequately met _____ or unmet _____

What would it take to meet it?

_____

_____

What is the first step toward getting it met?

_____

MEDITATION_____

Need met _____

How and by whom or what?

_____

_____

Need inadequately met _____ or unmet _____

What would it take to meet it?

_____

_____

What is the first step toward getting it met?

_____

WORSHIP/LITURGY_____
Need met _____

How and by whom or what?

_____

_____

Need inadequately met _____ or unmet _____
What would it take to meet it?

_____

_____

What is the first step toward getting it met?

_____

NATURE_____
Need met _____

How and by whom or what?

_____

_____

Need inadequately met _____ or unmet _____
What would it take to meet it?

_____

_____

What is the first step toward getting it met?

_____

DEVOTIONAL/INSPIRATIONAL READING_____
Need met _____

How and by whom or what?

_____

_____

Need inadequately met _____ or unmet _____

What would it take to meet it?

_____

_____

What is the first step toward getting it met?

_____

RETREATS/CONFERENCES_____

Need met _____

How and by whom or what?

_____

_____

Need inadequately met _____ or unmet _____

What would it take to meet it?

_____

_____

What is the first step toward getting it met?

_____

MUSIC_____

Need met _____How and by whom or what?

_____

_____

Need inadequately met _____ or unmet _____

What would it take to meet it?

_____

_____

What is the first step toward getting it met?

_____

TWELVE-STEP PROGRAMS_____

Need met _____

How and by whom or what?

_____

_____

Need inadequately met _____ or unmet _____

What would it take to meet it?

_____

_____

What is the first step toward getting it met?

_____

OTHER SPIRITUAL OR SUPPORT GROUPS_____

Need met _____

How and by whom or what?

_____

_____

Need inadequately met _____ or unmet _____

What would it take to meet it?

_____

_____

What is the first step toward getting it met?

_____

OTHER_____

Need met _____

How and by whom or what?

_____

_____

Need inadequately met _____ or unmet _____

What would it take to meet it?

_____

_____

What is the first step toward getting it met?

_____

CHAPTER NINE

Developing Your Recovery Plan

Dana, the beautiful seductress we met in Chapter Two, often characterizes her life today as the fulfillment of "the wish I never knew I had." What an apt description of the possibilities and potentials that await us—without our knowing it. Most of us human beings have wishes or dreams that fire our imaginations. Some dreams we think we can realize, but others we are quite sure we cannot. But then there are those dreams that await us in a place beyond our consciousness; these are the dreams that "blow our minds" when they are realized, for we cannot conceive of them ahead of time. They unfold before us as we take the next step on the road of self-discovery, of becoming the selves we can be.

Ironically, it can be our compulsions that put our feet on the pathway to self-discovery. When the emotional pain or the financial disaster or the physical illness we encounter is so devastating that it interrupts our lives as usual, we are receiving an invitation to pursue the "examined life." Usually what we find changes our lives in ways we could not have imagined.

As I pointed out in the introduction, there are several ways to read and engage this book. One is to casually stroll through the pages, just taking in information. Another is to read specifically to see if you find yourself mirrored anywhere. Yet another way is to read with a level of commitment that means you participate in the book as a program. You do the exercises, you reflect on the questions and you examine your own life in the light of the case histories and their accompanying explanations. If you are reading this book as an experience in personal growth and you are committed to making changes in your life that may open it up to becoming the fulfillment of the "wish you never knew you had," this chapter is particularly important for you. It is the culmination of the recovery process and of the work we have done in the previous chapters.

This chapter will provide a number of exercises, some written and some unwritten. Of course you will get the most from the chapter if you do the exercises, but only you can know what level of commitment you have to participating in the program the book provides. If you still aren't quite certain, our first exercise will help you determine how much time you currently spend on personal growth and how much time you would like to spend.

Determining Your Level of Commitment

If you don't know how you are currently spending your time each day or week, this exercise will help you clarify your time allocations. On a sheet of paper draw four pies, each one about the size of an upside-down coffee cup. In the first pie, section off pieces that represent your time expenditures for a typical day of your life (or for today). How much time do you spend working? How much time sleeping? How much at meals? How much with your family and friends? How much watching television? How much on personal growth, reading, meditation, etc.? How much on other things? Allot percentages to the pieces of your pie based on the relative size of each.

Now move to the second pie. Remembering your needs assessment exercise from Chapter Eight, section off the pieces of this pie to represent the time allotments you would *like* to give to each activity in your day. Now compare the two pies, the one that represents your life as it is and the one that represents your life as you would like it to be. What differences do you notice, and how could you set about making the time allotments represented by the second pie a reality? What time have you allotted for personal growth?

Now, if you choose, repeat the sectioning procedure with the next two pies, this time for week-long segments of your time. Do the weekly percentages surprise you? What percentage of a week do you spend sleeping? Working? Playing? Devoting to your personal growth?

One of the most frequent complaints I hear from people is "I don't have time." This exercise helps you make a realistic assessment of your time so that you know whether your complaint is valid or whether you are using it to avoid doing certain things. If you are committed to working the program this books suggests, on a regular daily basis you will need to spend ten minutes in the morning and ten minutes in the evening on the program. Do you have the time? Are you willing to take it?

Another question we need to ask ourselves as we look at a recovery program is this: How dedicated am I to changing? Change involves a certain amount of discomfort and disequilibrium. Are you willing to feel uncomfortable temporarily? Are you willing to change some thought patterns? If you are not, then a program for change will probably not be successful for you. If we are committed to change, there will be times when we may feel not only discomfort, but also pain. A painless recovery is usually not a recovery at all. We may experience fear, sadness, anger—all the feelings we talked about in Chapter Four. It can help us to remember that all these feelings are appropriate to change and that change most likely will not occur without them.

The Fear and Excitement of Change

A very simple exercise that can show us how uncomfortable change usually is involves our daily routine and body motions. Try several of the following and notice how you feel.

1. If you usually turn on the water tap with your right hand, turn it on with your left hand.

2. If you usually get out of bed on the left side, get out of bed on the right side.

3. If you usually answer the phone by saying "Hello," answer by saying "Hi" or "Jones residence."

4. If you usually have coffee at 6:00 a.m., try having tea at 7:00 a.m.

5. If you usually walk a mile in the morning, walk a mile in the evening.

The kind of discomfort we feel at any change, even a minor one, may be magnified many times when we are trying to change an entire behavior pattern, especially one as pervasive as a compulsion. We need to have respect for the magnitude of the step we are taking if we engage in a program for change.

It is important to remember that change occurs on two levels, in two arenas—inwardly and outwardly. Usually the inner changes come first and are manifested later in outward changes. Often I hear people say, "I've been in therapy for a year, and I still don't see any changes in my life." It may have taken thirty-five years for a pattern to become entrenched. Expecting sweeping outward changes immediately may be unrealistic and can set us up to sabotage our own progress.

Sometimes the seeds of change are sown slowly, but one day we wake up and see an abundant harvest. In other cases, changes are more immediately apparent and take place more steadily. Each person grows and changes differently, at a different rate. But usually the inner change is occurring without our seeing overt signs of it, and then we see the outer changes later. Just as a seed grows beneath the ground, hidden from our scrutiny, so internal change happens imperceptibly at first, taking its own time to appear outwardly.

Sometimes, however, people decide to adopt the very time-honored and usually psychologically sound principle of acting "as if." They may act courageous when they feel fearful and would usually display fearful or timid behavior. By acting "as if" they are courageous, they may walk themselves through the fear, eventually finding that their feelings and their inner disposition have changed to be in accord with their chosen behavior. Don't be surprised if change comes about for you through changing both your attitudes and your behavior.

As we have noted previously, leaving our compulsive behavior patterns behind frees up energy, resources and options that were unavailable to us before, when we were engaging in our compulsions. What has been variously called the "blank slate," the "fertile void," or "uncharted territory" by psychologists, therapists and philosophers is now open before us, and we can perceive it either as a gaping hole or as a wonderful clearing that gives us space to do what we've always longed to do—or what we didn't even know we longed to do. New choices will suddenly present themselves.

Choices inevitably bring both excitement and fear—excitement about all the wonderful possibilities that await us and fear of the possibility of failure, of the unknown, of being responsible for the decisions that only we can make. Prisoners who have done their time have sometimes been known to commit other crimes so they could go back to prison, which represented the security of the known and familiar. All the choices that faced them in the wide-open world were just too overwhelming. If we are going to change, we need to know that life will present us with more choices, not fewer, more decisions, not fewer. Life won't get easier, but it will certainly be filled with more vitality and more excitement than we have known before.

Assessing the Benefits of Change

Before we list the steps of our recovery programs, it may be helpful for us to do some preliminary exercises to help us assess the benefits of change—giving up our compulsions—as opposed to staying as we are, driven by our compulsions.

WHAT YOUR COMPULSION COSTS YOU

The first exercise is adapted from programs that work with addictions. On a sheet of paper, make a list of what your compulsion costs you. The following questions may help you discover what toll your compulsion is taking on your life.

1. What does your compulsion cost you in money?

2. What does your compulsion cost you in time?

3. What does your compulsion cost you in resources (that is, your talents, interests and capabilities)?

4. What does your compulsion cost you in energy (physical, emotional, mental and spiritual)?

5. What does your compulsion cost you in health and well-being?

6. What does your compulsion cost you in relationships?

7. What does your compulsion cost you professionally?

The answers to these questions will vary from person to person, but also from compulsion to compulsion. Gambling is more likely to waste money, while caretaking is more likely to take emotional and physical energy. Speeding is more likely to take a toll on one's health and well-being, while overexercising may cost a great deal in terms of both time and perhaps relationships (as it did Dave in Chapter Five, who had trouble keeping dates because he was always in the gym). However, a specific compulsion may be costing you more than you realize in all seven areas.

WHAT GIVING UP YOUR COMPULSION COULD SAVE YOU

Looking at your answers to the above questions, calculate what you would have available for yourself—what you would save, in a sense—if you gave up your compulsion. What would you have that you don't have now in terms of the following:

1. Money

2. Time

3. Resources

4. Energy

5. Health and well-being

6. Relationships

7. Career satisfaction and potential

LIFE WITH AND WITHOUT YOUR COMPULSION

This exercise is to be done a little later in your recovery process when you are moving away from engaging in the compulsion. It involves doing what people in recovery programs call "research."

For two weeks, keep a running list of observations you make about life with your compulsion and life without your compulsion. Record these on a sheet of paper with two columns labeled "Life with the Compulsion" and "Life without the Compulsion." At the end of two weeks, write a paragraph summarizing the differences between life with your compulsion and life without it. How do the differences make you feel? Do you feel that you have unmet needs in life without the compulsion—needs that were previously met by the compulsion? If so, what are they? How could they be met in some other way?

WHAT WILL YOUR LIFE BE LIKE IN FIVE YEARS?

On a sheet of paper, make two columns labeled "What Will My Life Be Like in Five Years with My Compulsion?" and "What Will My Life Be Like in Five Years without My Compulsion?" Using data from the previous two exercises, project into the future, five years from now. If, like Patti, you spend $800 every three months at the casinos, what will your financial picture look like? What will your budget look like if you continue to spend $3,200 every year for five years at Atlantic City? If you give up your compulsion, what will you be able to do in five years with an "extra" $16,000?

Your Recovery Program

The following steps make up the recovery program you will need to follow if you want to move toward living a compulsion-free life. You will need to tailor your plan to your individual needs and goals; however, in my experience, a workable plan usually includes all of the following steps. Steps one through six are explained in this chapter. Step seven will be explained more fully in Chapter Ten.

1. Identify and define your compulsion.

2. Identify your feelings.

3. Locate your feelings in your body. Where do you feel them? Check your body for clues.

4. Become aware of your thought patterns. What is the probable unconscious fantasy your compulsion acts out?

5. Create a positive thought-change statement.

6. Create a daily strategic plan to use at times when you are vulnerable to your compulsion.

7. Create a support system.

IDENTIFYING YOUR COMPULSION

Chapters Two and Three explained how to identify and define your compulsion and gave examples of tracking the cycle and pattern of a compulsion. By now you should have a clear idea how to identify and define your compulsion. Identification and definition are the essential first step in treating any discomfort. Without a name and a diagnosis for our malady, we don't know what treatment it requires.

IDENTIFYING YOUR FEELINGS

My personal and professional experience has taught me a lot about where feelings come from. Today, helping professionals often debate about what came first, the thought or the feeling. If we change the feeling, will the thought follow, or vice versa? It is my belief, based on my practice, that we need to work on the feelings first (if they are consciously accessible), and then the thoughts.

A baby doesn't think "Nobody's feeding me." He just feels hungry; he cries due to the feeling of hunger. The baby responds to the environment on a feeling level. Later, however, when he is able to formulate thoughts and then to conceptualize, he may acknowledge the hunger he is feeling by thinking about the hunger, why he is hungry, who is responsible for his hunger and so on. These thoughts—and distortions arising from them—may create more feelings, some of which are not in accordance with reality at all.

A small child is not unlike a movie camera that films what is going on in the environment. The child, like a camera, records what's happening, and once the events form images on the film, the movie projector projects those same images outward. Whatever is on the film gets projected onto the screen—including the distortions resulting from our family trance—and so we see this same movie wherever we go. Until we make a new film, one that is less reflective of distortions, we'll see the old one over and over.

One of the things that can be confusing in working with feelings is discerning whether we're feeling something as a result of taking an accurate reading of our environment or as a result of projecting an old image onto the environment, distorting what's happening in the outer world. Sometimes we pick up what's happening intuitively; at other times we project our own distorted image onto a perfectly benign situation.

Working on ourselves and paying keen attention to inner and outer signals will help us to hone our internal mechanisms and let us know whether some of our feelings need to be reeducated in accordance with a more accurate picture of reality than the one we had as a child. If we feel guilty every time we do well, for example, our feelings will need to be reeducated. These feelings undoubtedly come from early experiences in which we were made to feel bad for surpassing someone else. Lois, the woman in Chapter Six who "failed for father" and got the shakes after doing well on an exam, is a good example.

In addition to using Chapter Four, *Encountering Your Feelings,* to help you with step two, you may also want to keep a journal of your feelings. Just as people working on their overeating may write down everything they eat in a daily record and compulsive spenders may enter every expenditure in a financial log, so you may want to jot down your feelings in a journal at the end of the day. Or, if you want to do some research about your feelings, you may do a morning check-in and then a progressive observation that lets you know any strong emotional reactions you had (positive or negative), whether they were appropriate to the situation or were overreactive, what in the situation triggered those strong feelings and how you might react to a similar situation the next time. Notice any resentments and feelings of being slighted, excluded, laughed at or manipulated. Notice what made you feel happiest all day. Was it a smooth or rocky day in terms of your feelings? If you decide to keep your feelings journal for a number of weeks, or even months, you will have enough material to start to see cycles and patterns in your feelings. Dana, for example, almost always felt abandoned by the third day that she hadn't heard from a lover.

LOCATING YOUR FEELINGS IN YOUR BODY

Remembering what I have already said about humans as mind/body systems, we need to be aware of our bodies as clue-givers about our feelings and our overall state of being. We don't feel feelings only in our minds; we feel them in our bodies as well. We get "butterflies" in our stomachs when we are nervous, we get "heartaches" when we are lonely, we may experience back pain when we are overburdened, and headaches often signal mental overload.

Keeping in mind that this is not an art contest, draw a fairly large outline of your body on some newsprint or poster board. Over a period of three of four days, attempt to record your feelings, and see if you can locate them in your body. Choosing a different color to symbolize each feeling, at the end of the day draw in with colored markers or pens the feelings you recall locating in specific body areas. If you were feeling light and happy, you might mark the heart area yellow. Or if you were feeling nervous or angry, you might mark the stomach area orange or red. (A tightness in the chest and a constriction in the throat are other common locatable feelings, as are a stiff neck, aches in the joints, upper and lower back pain, heaviness in the legs and tingling in the hands and feet.) Keep this emotional picture of yourself in a prominent place, such as on the refrigerator door, to let it remind you of the reality of your feelings and the fact that they are locatable.

OBSERVING YOUR BODY FOR CLUES

Some programs downplay the role of the body in a whole-person recovery. As a way of cultivating body awareness, do the following exercise slowly, bringing to it as many powers of observation as you can.

Right now, without moving, notice how you're sitting (or standing or lying). Slow down your breathing and imagine yourself, in your mind's eye, stepping outside your body and observing yourself as you are sitting. What do you see? What do you notice about the way you're sitting? Do you look comfortable? Relaxed? Energized? Depressed? Observe yourself as acutely as if you were watching someone else.

Now go inside your body, still breathing slowly, noticing the rhythm of your breath as it goes in and out, in and out. Notice if your rib cage is expanding; notice if you're holding your chest tightly; notice if you allow your breath to fill your entire torso. Imagine what it would feel like if your whole chest area were elastic and could expand almost infinitely as you breathe. Be aware if there is tension or pain in your body as you breathe. Notice your general mood as you sit there, slowly breathing in and out.

Now shift your body and be aware, again, of stepping outside yourself. As you continue slowly breathing, observe your body in its new position. Notice any subtle shifts in energy, mood or feeling. Do you see any differences? If so, what are they?

BECOMING AWARE OF YOUR THOUGHTS
AND NAMING YOUR FANTASY

Most of us are not aware of the power of our thoughts. We can start to notice their effect on us by trying on various thoughts and recording what happens. If you want to do an experiment with your thoughts, say aloud to yourself or a friend, "I can't do anything right," "I'm doomed to failure" or "My life is bleak and miserable," and watch a pall settle across the room. Conversely, see what happens if you say, "My best friend is coming to town," "I just won the lottery" or "My boyfriend just called to say he loves me." What differences did you notice between the reactions that resulted from the two different types of statements? What did your body language reveal in each case?

To become more aware of your thoughts, take ten minutes to write down, on several blank sheets of paper, every thought that occurs to you as it occurs to you, in free association style. When the time is up, take five minutes to get up and walk around the room, consciously remembering to breathe. (Breathing, rather than holding our breath, keeps us open to an experience on a deeper, more feeling level.) After five minutes, return to what you wrote and underline all thoughts that enhance self-esteem and feelings of well-being in yellow and all thoughts that negate feelings of well-being in purple. Copy all the thoughts underlined in yellow onto one sheet(s) of paper, and copy all the thoughts underlined in purple onto another sheet(s) of paper. The list of positive thoughts might include such statements as these: "I remember the fun I had last night," "This room is comfortable," "This exercise is interesting," "The street noises remind me of my trip to Paris." The list of negative thoughts might include the following: "My stomach feels tight," "I wonder if Dave still has it in for me," "I'm afraid the brake job on the car is going to shoot the budget."

Now read the two lists aloud and notice any effects they have on you. Next, take each negative thought statement and rephrase it positively. For example, you might change "My stomach feels tight" to "I can relax my stomach tension by breathing slowly in and out." Or you might change "I'm afraid the brake job is going to shoot my budget" to "I'm confident that I'll have enough money to pay for my brake job." Now read this last list aloud slowly, while consciously breathing, and notice any reactions your body may register.

CREATING A POSITIVE
THOUGHT-CHANGE STATEMENT

We may not be aware of it, but our thoughts are pivotal in dealing with compulsions. We need to note our thoughts, just as we note our feelings, to find out what they tell us about our belief systems. Our belief systems support our compulsions at some level, so if we are to make changes in our lives by giving up our compulsions, we must be willing to change our belief systems by making changes in our thoughts. When we are in the process of changing negative thoughts into positive ones, "I can't's" into "I can's," we need to be careful to avoid using negatives in our affirmative statements. For example, changing "I'm worried that I can't pay my bills" into "Don't worry; be confident" does not help us develop a positive attitude because it still focuses on the negative by using "Don't." What we know about the unconscious tells us that it does not register negatives. Therefore, "Don't worry" is received as "Worry!" A better alternative is "Relax; you are safe in the world today." Telling our unconscious "Don't worry" is similar to telling a child "Don't put beans up your nose" or telling ourselves "Don't think about a pink elephant." One reason diets generally do not work is that they keep an overeater's attention even more intently focused on food because of all the "don't's."

Becoming aware of our thoughts and our belief systems, as well as a close reading of the material in Chapters One through Eight, can help us to uncover the probable unconscious fantasy that is crucial to our compulsion. Following is a list of common compulsions, a probable unconscious fantasy that underlies each, and a positive thought-change statement.

Compulsion	Probable Fantasy	Positive Statement
Work	I can endure long hours under difficult conditions, and then I'll receive approval.	I can relax and enjoy life and still be loved.
Success	I can be better than others, and then I'll receive validation.	I can be loved just for myself.
Spending	I can buy my way to emotional contentment.	I can find out what my emotional needs are and fulfill them.
Neatness	I can maintain stability by putting all aspects of my world into perfect order.	I can learn to appreciate the subtleties and paradoxes of life, thus adding richness to my experience.

Exercise	I can have a perfect body, and then I will be loved.	I accept my body just as it is, knowing I will still be loved if it's not perfect.
Rescuing	I can take care of everyone's problems and therefore be loved.	I can attend to my own needs and still be loved.

The preceding are examples only of *probable* unconscious fantasies. No one but you can ascertain what your real unconscious fantasy is—and it may take a long time for you to discover it. Following the program in this book may help you become aware of your fantasy, but you may also find that you need other tools, such as a competent therapist, a trusted friend or a support group. When the realization strikes, you will know it; it will fit—and it will explain a lot of other people's behaviors and attitudes toward you and observations about you that may never have made sense before. But the unconscious does not yield up its secrets until it is ready. Sometimes a dream may give you a clue to something you need to know, for dreams are the language of the unconscious.

CREATING A DAILY STRATEGIC PLAN

Although some components of a daily strategic plan will remain constant no matter what the compulsion, the strategies themselves will vary considerably from person to person. Each individual in the process of changing will need to create strategies that specifically respond to his or her own needs.

For example, Jerry, the man in Chapter Four who was driven to "beat the clock," would look over his schedule in the morning, see he had a dentist's appointment at 1:00 p.m. and, instead of leaving the usual half-hour before the appointment, consciously allot one hour, noting that he must leave the house at noon. He would line up a support person he could check in with to make this strategy more "real," and he would call this person at 11:45 to report that he was about ready to leave.

Some Examples

Jerry would state aloud any anxiety he might be experiencing about making this change in his routine and then be prepared to notice his feelings—and their location in his body—as he drove to the dentist's office. He would also be aware of the monologue going on in his head. He would notice what happened when he got to the dentist's office twenty minutes ahead of time. Did he feel jittery and nervous? Did he pace? Could he identify what was so frightening about this empty time? This was a good time for Jerry to take out his thought-change statement and to read it ten times to himself, slowly, while remembering to breathe.

At the end of the day, Jerry would record this episode and any other data of note in his feelings journal, evaluate his strategy and report to a trusted friend what had happened. He needed to remind himself that every forward step he took, even if it was merely a step in awareness, was a success. I have sometimes heard people castigate awareness, saying that it doesn't change anything. But it can be a powerful tool in building the foundation for change.

Jerry would record his success and then reward himself—perhaps by hearing a friend's supportive words, perhaps by planning a celebration lunch with friends after he had taken ten trips for which he had allowed ample time. As Jerry slowly built his awareness, maintaining contact with his feelings, his body clues, his thoughts, his positive statements, his exercises from this program and a support group, his awareness led to greater clarification, which refined his daily plan, his strategies and his successes.

For Susan, the woman in Chapter Four who always took handouts in her relationships and was involved with Frank, the mother's boy, part of the strategy involved learning to tolerate eye contact. She started practicing with a friend, then moved toward looking directly at co-workers, her boss or her family. Because she felt like a castoff who deserved no better than minimal attention, really engaging in an equal relationship with others was very threatening, for it broke her old, familiar pattern of feeling "less than" others. Practicing eye contact, including even two minutes for it in her daily plan, slowly built up Susan's ability to tolerate mutuality instead of inferiority.

Charlotte, the woman described in Chapter Four whose compulsion was "looking smart," included in her daily plan learning to tolerate wearing a pair of jeans for a little while each day. First she wore them in the house, then she wore them to go out to the mailbox and then she even wore them to go downtown. Bit by bit Charlotte learned to tolerate the tremendous anxiety that wearing something casual elicited in her. She noticed that the world did not fall apart and her brain did not deteriorate just because she didn't go to town in a designer suit.

For Janine, the jogger, an initial strategy was to cut down her running to four miles a day the first week, three miles a day the next week and so on. If she couldn't tolerate cutting down her exercise by a mile a week, then she cut down by a half mile—or whatever she could tolerate. For someone engaged in three sports a day, a strategy might be to cut back to two sports a day, and eventually to one.

One of the first strategies Harry, the movie binger, engaged in was to sit down with me to literally draw out, block by block, a map of all the movie theaters within ten blocks of his apartment.

Vanessa, the charge-card buyer from Chapter One, gave all her credit cards to a friend for safekeeping for a year and, until she had learned to educate herself about what was appropriate spending, she always took a friend shopping with her so that she could have someone she trusted to ask how realistic she was being in her purchasing.

As you may recall, Joanne, the rescuer described in Chapter Three, had a list of topics ready next to her phone so that she could have self-directed conversations with her mother that were not about her sick father or the dire financial situation at home.

Noting Times of Vulnerability and What Triggers Your Compulsion

In creating strategies, it is important for each individual to note his or her times of vulnerability to the compulsion. A good way to assess when these times occur in your life is to refer to Chapter Three on the cycle and pattern of compulsions and then to sit down with a piece of paper and mentally go through your day, noting what times are most likely to produce stress and anxiety, times that could set off a compulsive behavior to soothe the tension.

Refer to what you learned about triggers in Chapter Three. What people, places and things might you encounter today that could set off your compulsion? If possible, in the early stages of change avoid these people, places and things until you have built up more awareness, strength, supports and strategies.

If it is not possible to avoid them, then make sure you have a plan that includes several options for support. Take your positive thought-change statement with you wherever you go. Have a list of phone numbers of supportive people you can call. Make a cassette tape you can play for yourself (a particularly good strategy if you are going home to visit, especially on holidays). Write yourself a supportive letter from your inner benevolent parent and carry it with you. Carry a symbolic or special object with you in your pocket or handbag that you can touch or look at in times of stress. Enter stressful situations as if you were an investigative reporter gathering facts about yourself in relationship to your circumstances and relationships (you might take mental notes and transfer them to your feelings journal later).

Creating Your Daily Plan

Having become familiar with the exercises in this chapter, having read the material and answered the questions in this book and having created some practical strategies appropriate to you and your compulsive behavior, now write out a daily plan for ten minutes in the morning and ten minutes in the evening. Remember, if you are not committed to change, do not attempt to make and execute a plan. You will only end up discouraged. Remember, too, to take your recovery work step by step. The quickest way to sabotage your progress is to attempt too much too soon. Remember that *every* step is an important step and that you need to reward yourself for your progress. Be compassionate toward yourself.

A. Morning Plan

A typical ten-minute morning plan might include the following:

1. Slowly read your positive thought-change statement aloud ten times, remembering to breathe in order to feel the benefit of your positive thought. Not breathing blocks the reception of your positive thought.

2. Read the list of losses in your life that you previously compiled as a result of observing the effect of your compulsion on your life. This will remind you why you are making changes: You no longer want these losses in your life.

3. Reflect on your day and visualize yourself going through the day, noting times when you expect to be vulnerable to your compulsion.

4. Choose at least two strategies from the ones you have created to help you get through times of anxiety or stress without resorting to your compulsion. Note the abundance of possible strategies that exist (reread the strategies in the preceding paragraphs if necessary). Make sure that you carry with you anything you need to have for your strategies—your positive thought-change statement, your phone list, a special object or a tape and tape player.

B. Evening Plan

A typical evening plan might include two or three of the following. Remember that it's best to limit your time to ten minutes or less; otherwise you may be overwhelmed by the time commitment and sabotage your growth.

1. Write in your journal, noting any observations you've made about your feelings, body clues, thoughts, times of vulnerability and strategies.

2. Evaluate your strategies. Do you need to change or refine them? If so, how?

3. Read through your positive thought-change statement ten times, consciously breathing.

4. Call a trusted friend or member of a support group to talk for a minute or two about your day.

5. Note your success today, remembering that awareness is a success. Decide how you could reward yourself, either now or later. An appropriate award might be a phone call to a special friend, a bubble bath or taking time to read a chapter in a favorite book—anything that would be out or the ordinary for you that would affirm your success today.

Remember, the reward should be nourishing, not debilitating. A movie binger cannot reward himself by going to the movies! A spender cannot reward herself by charging a new outfit! A good test of the appropriateness of a reward is to ask yourself this: Does the reward enhance my self-esteem or detract from my self-esteem?

Handling Inevitable "Slips"

Inevitably, we all make "slips"—that is, we fall back into some aspect of the behavior we are trying to change. Instead of berating yourself, however, take the "slip" as an opportunity to do "research." Examine the incident without judging yourself, talking your experience over with a trusted friend, writing it down in your journal, sharing it with a support group or reflecting on it with a therapist. Use the experience to clarify the awareness you have already gained. Some of our slips teach us more than some of our successes. It's all grist for the mill, so don't waste time punishing yourself. Just keep on keeping on.

CREATING A SUPPORT SYSTEM

This aspect of a personal recovery program is so significant and many-faceted that we will be devoting an entire chapter to it (Chapter Ten).

A Review:
Dana's Recovery Plan

To review and synthesize the information presented in this chapter so far, it may be helpful to go through the recovery steps once again using Dana, perhaps our best-developed example, as a case in point. Dana's initial recovery plan was as follows:

1. Identify and define your compulsion.
Seduction.

2. Identify your feelings.
Abandonment, panic, anxiety and fear.

3. Locate your feelings in your body.
Neck pain from nervousness, occasional nausea when no contact has been made with a lover, sweaty palms, a pounding heart from panic and anxiety, the shakes as I begin to make changes.

4. Become aware of your thought patterns. What is the probable unconscious fantasy your compulsion acts out?
If I dazzle men with my sexuality, I can be powerful and get all the attention and things I need.

5. Create a positive thought-change statement.
I can be loved for my true self.

6. Create a daily strategic plan to use at times when you are vulnerable to your compulsion.
Read positive thought-change statement while breathing.
Note dinner engagement with a new date.
On the date, keep my phone number to myself; get my date's number instead.
Call Joan if necessary; carry the numbers of two friends I can call.

Play the tape I have made as I drive to the supper club.
At the end of the day record my feelings for five minutes.
Repeat my positive thought-change statement ten times.
Do my compassion exercise. (I'll describe this later.)

Of course this plan changed as Dana moved along in her process of awareness, clarification and recovery.

Your Recovery Plan

Now, using Dana's example as a model, fill in the following data for yourself.

1. Identify and define your compulsion.

_____

2. Identify your feelings.

_____

3. Locate your feelings in your body. Where do you feel them? Check your body for clues.

_____

_____

4. Become aware of your thought patterns. What is the probable unconscious fantasy your compulsion acts out?

_____

_____

5. Create a positive thought-change statement.

_____

6. Create a daily strategic plan to use at times when you are vulnerable to your compulsion.

_____

_____

_____

7. Create a support system. (Fill in after reading Chapter Ten.)

_____

_____

Creating
and Maintaining
a Support System

"Lean on me when you're not strong," runs a line from a popular song written a few years ago that has particular significance for me. And for those of us who are getting over any malady—emotional, physical or spiritual—leaning on someone or something is crucial. But we must be very careful who or what it is—and how long we lean. Those of us who are recovering from compulsions leaned on our compulsions for years, and they were always there when we needed them. The problem was that the "support" these compulsions offered was insubstantial and illusive, and we obtained this support at a price that eventually proved too costly.

Support comes in two forms—short-term and long-term. Short-term support is what we need when we first start making changes in our lives, when we are in transition. This kind of support may include emotional first aid. The support we need for the short term is often like that a crutch gives a broken leg. A leg heals only if it receives the appropriate support, if we take care of it, if we don't walk on it too soon. On the other hand, if we use the crutch indefinitely our leg will become more and more spindly, lose more and more muscle tone and become weaker and weaker. The longer we wait to walk, the harder it becomes to use the leg.

The daily strategic plans we initially set up to work on living without compulsive behavior can usually be seen as short-term support. There comes a time when the positive thoughts and the rituals we have created for ourselves have become such a natural part of us that we don't need to go through all our coping strategies on a daily basis.

Long-term support, unlike the appropriate, necessary crutch of short-term support, consists of the ongoing, healthy life patterns we create to sustain us in a new way of being. These patterns are related to the normal needs of human beings we discussed and charted in Chapter Eight, *Assessing Your Needs,* and involve such things as relaxing and creating balance, learning to play and celebrate, experiencing the benevolent parent part of ourselves and treating our inner child with compassion and tenderness, setting goals and boundaries, forming a relationship with a higher power or a source of spiritual support and serenity, drawing on the support of other people and using resource materials.

Learning to Relax and Create Balance

There are abundant resources on learning to relax (some of them are listed at the end of this chapter). However, several exercises, guidelines and techniques I have found helpful with clients, both individually and in groups, include the following:

1. Close your eyes and begin breathing slowly and rhythmically. As you relax and settle into a steady rhythm, concentrate on the phrase "I can" as you inhale, and "relax" as you exhale. Repeat this for five to ten minutes.

2. Close your eyes and visualize a safe place, the safest place you can think of. It might be a lovely beach, a secure fortress, a forest in autumn. Imagine spending an hour in this safe place with no intrusions, no anxiety. What do you see, touch, taste, smell, hear and inwardly experience in this place?

3. Recall a scene in a movie, play or book in which someone behaved as you would like to behave in a stressful situation. What did they do that you have never thought of doing? How did they turn a negative situation into a positive action? How could you adapt this behavior to stressful situations in your own life? Use the image of this person to help you through the next anxious or stressful incidents you experience.

Learning to Play and Celebrate

We talked about this topic in Chapter Eight, but many of us who have no clue about how to play may need some specific hints. Although we can engage in imaginative play by ourselves, being playful is enhanced by being with others. Following are some suggestions for playing alone and with others that have worked for my clients. The suggestions listed under "Adult Play" are meant to develop your adult capacity to be playful, while the suggestions under "Spontaneous Play" are deliberately childlike, designed to help you feel the spontaneity of a five- or six-year-old.

It is important to begin to learn to play by engaging in an activity that you will actually be able to enjoy. Play, especially certain types of spontaneous play, can be very frightening because it can seem "childish," which means having less power and control. Therefore, it may be important to begin to learn to play by engaging in "adult" types of play such as those listed in section A below. Then you can gradually proceed, if you wish, to the more purely spontaneous activities listed in section B.

A. Adult Play

• If you are overly conscientious on the job, take an afternoon off to go to the movies or take in a ball game.

• If you always plan your vacations to a "T," leave one or two days unplanned and see what you can spontaneously find to do or see.

• If you always arrange a date with your spouse, mate or lover ahead of time for a specific event, call to say that you'll be picking him or her up in two hours for a surprise evening. Then do what you feel like doing right then.

• If you always go to classical music concerts, try going to a concert of jazz or folk music.

• If you consistently save and conserve, never indulging yourself with whimsical expenditures, allow yourself to take a moderate sum of money (perhaps twenty or thirty dollars) to "blow" on a nonpractical gift for yourself.

B. Spontaneous Play

• Sculpt a figure out of modeling clay or play dough.

• Take a bubble bath with children's toys.

• Draw a scene with finger paints.

• Play charades with a partner.

• Tell an add-on story with a partner, each of you adding a few sentences until an unpredictable story has been woven.

• Stage a shadow puppet scene with a partner.

• Go to the zoo, the circus or an amusement park.

• With a partner, paint faces on each other using water-soluble face paint.

Experiencing Your Benevolent Parent and Inner Child

Both of the exercises below focus on the child, but in paying attention to the child we learn to become parental, perhaps in a way in which we were never parented as children.

1. Close your eyes, and in your mind's eye look at yourself as you were when you were eighteen. What are your feelings? Do you feel compassionate toward that young adult? Now move backward, to when you were sixteen, fourteen, twelve, ten. Do you feel compassionate toward that teenager, that adolescent, that child? Now move further backward in time, looking at yourself at the ages of eight, six, four, two, one, nine months, six months, three months, as a newborn.

What age was this child when you first felt the stirrings of compassion for him or her? Stop and concentrate on the face of the child at that age. Look at the child with compassion, with feeling for what the child was going through, for the lessons the child was learning, for any pain the child endured. Notice any memories that may surface from around this age.

If you are unable to feel any compassion for your inner child of the past at any age, then you probably received few expressions of compassion when you were growing up. You can now choose to go back and rewrite your compassionless life script by consciously selecting a trusted friend or support person who can express compassion toward you. Until we receive compassion from another, we cannot give it to ourselves or others.

2. Choose a photograph, preferably a large one, of yourself as a child. Place this photograph in a prominent place or in a location where you spend a lot of time—on a desk, a dresser or even a computer stand. Whenever you pass the photograph, sit down at the desk or stand in front of the dresser, greet this child. Speak gently to her, and inquire about her well-being. By paying attention to our concrete image of ourself as a child, by consciously and attentively cultivating contact, we will give a priceless gift to our own inner child—loving attention and concern. We are not so different from flower gardens: Without attention, we wither and wilt; with attention, we flourish and grow.

Setting Goals and Creating Boundaries

This aspect of our growth is so specific to the individual that it may be best to give a few examples as guidelines. For example, as Dana, the seductress, learned to place more attention on her own life and priorities, she found that there were lots of empty spaces her seduction ritual had previously filled. She eventually discovered that she had an interest in travel, in foreign cultures and in business. With a lot of support from friends and from me, Dana began to entertain an idea that seemed out of reach at first: owning her own business.

By first setting a goal, we were able to work backwards to increasingly specific steps she could take toward that goal, such as taking a course on import/export businesses, subscribing to a trade magazine and attending a couple of conferences, locating friends or acquaintances with some knowledge of import/export businesses and making lists of contacts.

The small tasks were endless, but Dana and I set up goals each week, and she faithfully reported to me at each succeeding session which tasks had been completed and which ones were ongoing. As she was able to build confidence by actually completing more and more of the tasks on her list, she was able to apply for a business loan, rent an office space and set up shop. Today she travels around the world, combining her love of adventure with her ability to autonomously make a living.

Patti, who overspent at the casino, also discovered after giving up her gambling compulsion that she could either fill the emptiness of her compulsion-free life with another debilitating behavior—or she could devote herself to achieving a worthwhile goal. Choosing to regard her new "blank slate" as an opportunity rather than a chasm, Patti found that she did have a dream—to own her own home.

She began with small steps indeed. Because fulfilling this dream seemed impossible and brought up so much anxiety, Patti set goals, with my help, that were manageable and designed to create a series of successes for herself. She began by reading the real estate section of the Sunday paper for five minutes only each Sunday for about a month. Then she began clipping one or two ads each week and bringing them to me. The idea of actually calling a real estate agent at this point was too intimidating.

Together Patti and I began to make a list of things she would like to have in a home. Because she wasn't used to making decisions and setting goals, the process was painstaking at first. Patti didn't know what she wanted; she only knew what she didn't want. She didn't want a ranch-style home; she didn't want ten bedrooms or one bedroom; she didn't want a brick exterior. Bit by bit as we refined her list of "don't want's" we began to get a picture of what she did want.

Eventually, with list in hand and trembling like a leaf, Patti took a friend and approached her first real estate agency. Two years and a lot of hard work later, Patti owns her dream house—on a lake. With all the money she saved since she quit her compulsion, she managed to make a down payment on a home she could never have imagined buying. She has a flower garden, she has made her own draperies and she has set firm boundaries about when her family can and cannot visit her.

As long as Patti had been in her cycle of spending and gambling, as long as her emotional energy had been tied up by her family, there had been no room for goals and achievements of her own. Her life had been empty, metallic, hard. She had reminded me of a pinball imprisoned inside a machine, ricocheting around in response to the manipulations of someone else. Now Patti's life has more serenity, balance and nourishment. She has developed interests she never knew she had. She watches birds in the woods on her lot and knows all about perennial and annual plants. Her chaotic, unpredictable, limited life is now more orderly, rewarding and spacious.

Developing a Relationship with a Spiritual Source

Although we discussed this aspect of growth in Chapter Eight, I want to reiterate that each person needs to find his or her own way of relating to a spiritual source. For many people in the now-famous twelve-step programs, the concept and experience of a Higher Power is sustaining and guiding. For members of religious denominations, their worship services or church life meet their need for a spiritual source. For others, walks in nature, surfing in the ocean or lovingly tending a garden meet their need to experience a force or creative power that is larger than their own individual lives and personalities. They feel a sense of transcendence in the presence of beauty—in the stillness of a forest at dawn, in the majesty of a mountain peak at sunset, in the power of waves crashing on an ocean beach.

One client of mine who was a fisherman used to get up at 4:00 a.m. and go out to the lake to catch trout. Although I found it difficult to imagine this experience as a source of spiritual support for myself, as I listened to him I realized that for him, with his orientation, background and interests, sitting in the pre-dawn quiet waiting, watching and being still was an awe-inspiring experience that deeply fed him the way that meditation, sacred music or inspirational sermons feed other people.

Drawing on the Support of Others

Finding out what nourishes us and supports us and then setting about to make it a regular part of our lives is an important component of getting over any destructive behavior pattern, a component that requires the creation and maintenance of a support system for our new life patterns. Both short- and long-term support have two sources: ourselves and others.

I have sometimes heard a person moving from sickness to wellness, from a destructive lifestyle to a creative one, say, ''I can do it alone.'' Although I would never claim that it is *impossible* to recover from compulsions alone, I think that recovering alone is improbable. We are social creatures, and we rely on other human beings in ways that we don't even stop to think about. Not to draw on the real and invaluable support of others is to make tremendous emotional demands on ourselves, demands most of us aren't equal to. And even if we were equal to such demands, what is the cost of such self-sufficiency? Not drawing on the willing resources around us, isolating ourselves inside our own self-will, can drive us back into our compulsions—or sometimes drive us into equally destructive new compulsions—back into the sorts of illusions we used to live from, illusions that told us we could get along fine, just we and our compulsions. It didn't work then, and it probably won't work now. If we examine this ''self-sufficiency'' more deeply, we will probably discover underneath it a lack of compassion for ourselves, for our humanity, for our imperfection. We may need to go back and do the exercises earlier in this chapter to develop compassion for our inner child.

Drawing on resources provided by others, however, is not a substitute for developing our own inner resources. We need to do both at the same time. If we do, we will discover that they complement each other in wonderful ways. We may share a book we've been reading, an exercise we've been doing or a strategy we've been practicing with a friend or a support group member and find that it strikes a chord, enriching all of us.

The components of a human support system may include a therapist, trusted friends, acquaintances, a support group, a twelve-step program and a higher power or spiritual source.

A THERAPIST

I want to issue a warning to people who are recovering from entrenched compulsions. As we saw in Chapter Four, often as we are making changes in our lives, buried feelings from the past start surfacing, causing discomfort, anger, sadness, fear and even panic. If at any time you find that you are being overwhelmed by negative feelings, call for help—and then locate a competent therapist who can help you through this scary and painful transition time. Initially you might call a trusted friend, someone on the phone list from your support group or twelve-step program, a community-service hotline that provides a listening ear and referrals, or a local minister, priest or rabbi.

If you feel you need a therapist, I suggest that you get three different names from people you trust or from referral agencies and then speak with each one, first on the phone, then in person. If you have negative feelings about the therapist, I suggest that you politely thank him or her for the consultation time, then move on to another interview. If you don't connect on an emotionally healing level with the therapist, perhaps it would be better not to see that therapist, no matter how impeccable his or her credentials. No one else but you can decide if you "connect" with a therapist. You may have to travel or put yourself out a bit to find and work with the right therapist for you. But remember, this is an investment in your life; don't sell it short.

Although you want a caring therapist, you don't want someone who is invasive and wants to rescue you. Nor do you want someone who sits in judgment upon you. You might want to make up a checklist of qualities that are important to you in choosing a therapist and then interview each of the three with your list in mind. Some people involved in twelve-step programs prefer a therapist with a "program" approach, but that is an individual preference.

FRIENDS AND ACQUAINTANCES

Friends and acquaintances range from a trusted confidante, mentor or guide with whom you share every step of your recovery pathway to casual acquaintances from the coffee shop, gym or civic organization you frequent. The network of people we have about us supports us in all kinds of ways, and as long as we can discern the appropriate way to relate to each person, we can gather nourishment from a variety of people.

In your daily strategic plan, it is important to locate at least one friend who is willing to act as a support for you during your transitional time. Often twelve-step programs urge each member to choose a *sponsor,* a person who is a bit further down the recovery road than you are and who can help you test the waters or catch you when you fall. The sponsor or guide may remain with you after you have left your "crutch" stage, but such a person is essential in the beginning. Many of my clients keep a phone list of trusted individuals they can call for help, support or advice or to share progress. A good place to keep a copy of the list is next to the phone or on the refrigerator. Always carry a copy with you in your wallet or handbag. You never know when a sympathetic ear will save the day.

One exercise that may help you concretely visualize your network of friends and acquaintances is as follows:

On a blank sheet of paper, draw a small circle in the center of the page to represent yourself. Now take another sheet of paper and cut out ten small triangles to represent men in your life and ten small circles to represent women in your life. Write a name on each triangle and each circle. Now start arranging the triangles and circles in varying degrees of proximity to the circle that represents you. If you have a strong connection to a person, put the triangle or circle representing him or her near to the circle that represents you. If you have only a casual and infrequent connection, put the triangle or circle farther away. When you are satisfied that you have put all the triangles and circles in their appropriate places, glue them to the paper.

Now look at the people who make up your network again. If your relationship with a person is currently clear, untroubled and positive, draw a solid line from you to the triangle or circle that represents that person. If the relationship is currently on a sour note, full of disturbance or anger, draw a dotted line from you to that person's triangle or square. Draw either dotted or solid lines from you to each of the twenty people in your network. What conclusions can you draw about your network as you reflect on the arrangement of circles and triangles? Would you like to make some changes in your system of friends and acquaintances?

Here are some questions for you to reflect on:

1. How many people are in your network? (I usually suggest that clients have at least fifteen people at this level.)

2. How many people are you close to? (I suggest that clients have at least three people they are close to.)

3. Answer the following questions if you have drawn dotted lines toward someone:

   a. Does that person have qualities that could be supportive to you?

b. Could you "repair" the relationship, considering the time and energy you have available?

c. If you choose not to repair the relationship, could you learn to accept it as it is?

Another question we often forget to ask ourselves in assessing the quality of our relationships when we are in recovery is this: How much opportunity does this relationship offer me to give as well as to receive? If we do all the taking and none of the giving, we may find ourselves in an unequal relationship, feeling resentful and "less than."

A SUPPORT GROUP

It was reported that approximately fifteen million Americans were involved in support groups of one kind or another in 1990. Every imaginable type of group, from the now-famous Alcoholics Anonymous and Overeaters Anonymous to groups for cross-dressers and manic-depressives, is now flourishing nationwide. It would appear that, no matter what your problem, concern or goal, there is a support group for you. However, just as you need to be careful in choosing a therapist, exercise the same caution and good judgment in locating an appropriate support group. Again, you may want to make a list of what you are looking for in a group. Or you may get a referral from a trusted friend, therapist or recovering member of a group. If possible, visit several groups to get a feeling for what goes on and whether the group would be helpful to you. Increasingly, therapists are running groups of their own, many based on twelve-step concepts but some not. At the end of this chapter, you will find a list of phone numbers and addresses that may be helpful if you are looking for a support group.

If you can't find a support group, create one. Many women, for example, have created support groups for "women who love too much," based on Robin Norwood's excellent guidelines at the back of her book of the same title. We are fortunate to be living at a time when we have a wealth of resources to choose from. If you have a specific concern, someone may well have written a book about it and provided guidelines for dealing with it. Some books that may be helpful to you are listed at the end of this chapter.

TWELVE-STEP PROGRAMS AND A HIGHER POWER

The twelve-step programs are now world-famous, with groups in nations around the globe. Founded by Bill W., a businessman who "bottomed out" because of his alcohol addiction, the groups are called "twelve-step" programs because they follow twelve sequential steps which group members regularly "work." Alcoholics Anonymous reputedly has the highest recovery rate for alcoholism among its members of any treatment program, and AA and the other anonymous groups are the backbone of a new way of life for many individuals.

I have successfully referred many clients to such groups and suggest that people with compulsive behaviors try to find groups that fit them. Adult Children of Alcoholics (ACOA) is often helpful for people encountering deep feelings for the first time. Al-Anon might prove helpful for compulsive rescuers, caretakers, people-eaters and crisis creators. Someone with a compulsive spending or charging behavior might seek help from Debtors Anonymous, while gamblers and chance takers might attend Gamblers Anonymous. Sex and Love Addicts Anonymous does not give out its phone number, but there is a central clearing-house number to call, again listed at the end of this chapter.

The twelve-step programs also rely on a "Higher Power," which program literature and sponsors can explain. Often people who have been spiritually abused—through rigid religious backgrounds or through crippling familial moral judgments—are deeply angered by the concept of a Higher Power and refuse to have anything to do with this aspect of a program. Those feelings are usually honored at meetings, in accordance with the recognition that everyone must begin with where he or she is now; no pressure is exerted for anyone to embrace a belief system.

Resources

Books, tapes, support groups, "anonymous" programs and other resources are an invaluable part of any support system. The following information is provided in the hope that you will take what you can and use it in your own recovery.

BOOKS

Benson, Herbert and Miriam Z. Klipper. *The Relaxation Response.* New York: Avon Books, 1976.

Borysenko, Joan. *Guilt Is The Teacher; Love Is the Lesson.* New York: Warner Books, 1990.

Bradshaw, John. *Home Coming: Reclaiming and Championing Your Inner Child.* New York: Bantam Books, 1990.

Fishel, Ruth. *The Journey Within: A Spiritual Path to Recovery.* Pompano Beach, Florida: Health Communications, 1987.

Friends in Recovery. *The Twelve Steps for Adult Children of Alcoholics and Other Dysfunctional Families.* San Diego, California: Recovery Publications, 1987.

Levine, Stephen. *A Gradual Awakening.* Garden City, New York: Anchor Books, Doubleday, 1979.

Norwood, Robin. *Women Who Love Too Much*. New York: Pocket Books, 1988.

Ram Dass. *Journey of Awakening; A Meditator's Guidebook*. New York: Bantam Books, 1985.

Subby, Robert. *Lost in the Shuffle; The Co-dependent Reality*. Pompano Beach, Florida: Health Communications, 1987.

Viorst, Judith. *Necessary Losses: The Loves, Illusions, Dependencies and Impossible Expectations that All of Us Have to Give Up in Order to Grow*. New York: Fawcett Gold Medal, 1986.

Wegscheider-Cruse, Sharon. *Choicemaking*. Pompano Beach, Florida: Health Communications, 1985.

TAPES
You should specify the title *and* the number of each tape when you order it from the address provided.

The Importance of Being Aware of Feelings
#JK105
Dharma Seed Tape Library
Box 66
Wendell Depot, MA 01380

Recovering Self-Esteem/Change—Not Chance
#1596G
Hazelden Educational Materials
Pleasant Valley Road
Box 176
Center City, Minnesota 55012-0176
(800) 328-9000

Relaxation—A Natural High
#1458G
Hazelden Educational Materials
Pleasant Valley Road
Box 176
Center City, Minnesota 55012-0176
(800) 328-9000

Training the Inner Child
#JK99
Dharma Seed Tape Library
Box 66
Wendell Depot, MA 01380

SUPPORT GROUPS
National Self-Help Clearinghouse
33 W. 42nd St.
New York, New York 10036
(212) 642-2944

ANONYMOUS PROGRAMS
Adult Children of Alcoholics (ACOA)
Central Service Board
P.O. Box 35623
Los Angeles, California 90035
(213) 464-4423

Al-Anon/Alateen Family Group Headquarters, Inc.
Madison Square Station
New York, New York 10010
(212) 683-1771

Debtors Anonymous
Check your local telephone directory.

Gamblers Anonymous
3255 Wilshire Blvd.
Los Angeles, California 90010
(213) 386-8789

Sex Addicts Anonymous (SAA)
P.O. Box 3038
Minneapolis, Minnesota 55403
(612) 871-1520

Sex and Love Addicts Anonymous (SLAA)
Augustine Fellowship
P.O. Box 119
New Town Branch
Boston, Massachusetts 02258
(617) 332-1845

OTHER
Hazelden Educational Materials
Pleasant Valley Road
Box 176
Center City, Minnesota 55012-0176
(800) 328-9000

Insight Meditation Society
Pleasant Street
Barre, Massachusetts 01005-9701
(508) 355-4378

Index